ADVANCED MOTORING

An exposition of the basis of advanced motoring techniques
compiled by the Institute of Advanced Motorists

Macdonald
Queen Anne Press

WITH THE INSTITUTE OF ADVANCED MOTORISTS

A Queen Anne Press **Book**

© Institute of Advanced Motorists 1977 and 1982

Jacket photograph: Tony Latham (Car by kind permission of the
Ford Motor Company)
Black and white photographs: Tony Latham
Line drawings: Ray and Corrine Burrows

First published April 1967
Reprinted May 1967
Revised edition September 1969
Reprinted November 1969
Reprinted June 1971
Reprinted June 1972
Reprinted October 1973
Reprinted October 1975
New edition September 1976
Reprinted November 1977
Reprinted September 1978
Revised and updated April 1982
Reprinted March 1985
Reprinted September 1986
First published in Great Britain by Queen Anne Press, a division of
Macdonald and Co (Publishers) Limited, 3rd Floor, Greater London
House, Hampstead Road, London NW1 7QX for the Institute of
Advanced Motorists Limited, IAM House, 359–365 Chiswick High
Road, London, W4 4HS.
Filmset, printed and bound in Great Britain by
Hazell Watson & Viney Limited,
Member of the BPCC Group,
Aylesbury, Bucks

CONTENTS

INTRODUCTION

It may be that, by international standards, British road users are a relatively safe group of people and our accident rate among the lowest in Europe, and this despite the fact that the weight of traffic is very heavy indeed. Even so, our safety performance on the roads is not exactly a matter for self-congratulation. The annual toll in terms of death and injury – not to mention the vast expense of it all – is still depressingly high.

What is happening to cut this toll? Firstly, the authorities regularly modify the rules and regulations governing road users in an effort to reduce the accident rate. And secondly, private groups from accident prevention organisations to vehicle manufacturers are continually striving to reduce the chances of an accident occurring in the first place, and to minimise its effects when the seemingly inevitable does occur. But this is not really enough, for almost no one is tackling the problem from the point of view of the driver.

This is where the Institute of Advanced Motorists comes in. It is our belief that the single most effective way open to any of us to reduce accidents is to press for a better standard of driving. The Institute was founded, with this aim in view, in 1956 at the suggestion of the then Minister of Transport. As a voluntary non-profit-earning charity, the Institute's primary purpose is to evaluate the driving standards of motorists who present themselves for the advanced test.

Passing or failing the test is not necessarily the main object: the evaluation, carried out by one of the Institute's examiners, all of whom hold a Class One Police driving certificate, is what counts. From this assessment the candidate can learn what is right in his driving and, much more important, what he should do to improve from a safety point of view. But even taking the advanced test implies a responsible attitude to good driving.

The Institute's method of driving, based on practices tried and tested by the police, is a clearly defined though not inflexible one. This method is set out in the pages of this book. Simply reading *Advanced Motoring* will, I believe, make you a better driver. But if you can put into practice on the road all that you can read here, you will become a thoroughly responsible motorist and a very safe driver indeed.

Major General E. H. G. Lonsdale, CB, MBE, MA, FCIT
Chairman, Institute of Advanced Motorists
Stogursey, Somerset

1

THE NEED FOR ADVANCED DRIVING

Every year something like 330,000 people in Britain are killed or injured on the roads, which is equivalent to the population of a city larger than Coventry. About 6,000 are killed, some 80,000 seriously injured and another 245,000 less seriously hurt. On average a road injury happens once every 99 seconds, and a death once every 75 minutes. In the time it takes to read this page, one person – and quite probably more – will be maimed in a road accident. Before long, there will be another death. A high proportion of those killed and injured are children and young people. In some groups – among young men, for instance – road accidents are the single most likely cause of death, outweighing all kinds of disease.

You may feel all these statistics have little to do with you personally but we would think that, since you have chosen to read this book, you have a responsible attitude towards road safety. Everyone has to face the fact that there is a good chance that you, or someone close to you, will be involved in a road accident. Of course, the future always looks brighter. All major manufacturers are making their cars safer and there is the prospect of better roads being built. There is also the increasing emphasis on road safety being taught in the classroom. But more effectively, we can act immediately and have a more significant effect on road safety than any of those other improvements. We can drive better, and the purpose of this book is to guide you in the ways of better driving.

This manual has been compiled by the Institute of Advanced Motorists to take drivers who have already passed the 'O'-level of the Government driving test on to the 'A'-level standard of advanced driving. The book is based on the driving methods used by the Institute's examiners, who are all former Class One police drivers. It doesn't reveal any short cuts to position you ahead of the next man in the traffic queue, for such tricks have no place in road safety. But it does contain the sum of years of experience in driving safely and with courtesy.

As proof of the success of the advanced driving techniques, take a look at the statistics. Since the Institute was founded in 1956, more than 250,000 drivers have taken the advanced driving test. More than half have passed and a survey by the Government's Transport and Road Research Laboratory shows that those who have been successful have, on average, a 25 per cent better accident record than those who fail and 50 to 70 per cent better than the general motoring public. They not only have fewer accidents but those in which they are involved tend to be less serious, according to the Laboratory. This proves that the Minister of Transport in 1956 who pressed for an organisation that would improve driving standards through an advanced driving test was correct in his judgement.

It was realised even then that the driver who proudly threw away his L-plates was only at the beginning of the learning process. The driving apprenticeship was complete and he was ready to develop his skill until he could reach the standard of master craftsman. Only then could he claim to be a safe and responsible motorist. This manual aims to pass on the information necessary to reach that standard. Naturally most of it concentrates on the driver, but there is much to be said, too, about making sure your car is fit for the road and this has been included. The *Highway Code* is a primer and a basis for learning; this book completes your driving course. Do remember, though, that the manual is a practical guide to driving, not a legal textbook. It does not seek to provide a detailed guide to the ever-changing mass of motoring rules and regulations.

2

PLANNING

A planned and systematic approach to everything you do behind the wheel is the basis of advanced driving. There is a set formula for all circumstances, although it is not inflexible since the driver must continually adapt to the changing situation. By keeping to the formula you can drive confident in the knowledge that you will be well equipped to cope with anything that happens on the road near you, and need never be caught out by an emergency, nor be panicked into making a wrong move. And you will be well on the way to achieving the active kind of road safety in which you anticipate the possible moves of others and avoid or prevent their accidents for them.

It is comforting to know that you minimise the chances of surprising other road users by sticking to a planned system of driving. Far too frequently a driver involved in an accident protests that he 'never expected the other chap to turn right/slow down/accelerate'. It does not matter whether the aggrieved party is right; better anticipation on his part, combined with a methodical, planned approach by the other driver would have prevented the accident happening at all. The system is described in detail throughout the rest of the book, as there is a driving plan to be put into practice for almost every situation.

Here is an example, which is worth quoting to illustrate the point. The system to be employed when turning, coming to a junction, or about to drive round a hazard such as roadworks is Course – Mirror – Signal – Brake – Gear – Acceleration. Remember it by bearing in mind that the initials stand for Can My Safety Be Given Away.

On the road, this mnemonic works out like this:
Course: Mentally select the correct course you intend to take.
Mirror: Check your mirror before changing course or altering speed.
Signal: Signal (if necessary) clearly and in good time to confirm your

intention to change course. Remember that clear signals assist all road users, including pedestrians.

Brake: Apply the brake when the car is travelling on a straight path to ensure correct road speed for a lower gear selection if required for maximum car control.

Gear: Select the gear required according to the severity of the hazard in order to arrive at the hazard travelling at the correct speed, with the correct gear engaged, and on the right part of the road.

Acceleration: Gentle acceleration at first, according to road and traffic conditions, and if safe to proceed more progressive acceleration can be applied.

Try 'commentary driving' while you are getting used to this system, even when you have reached that state and just want a running check on your standard. Simply give a running commentary to yourself on what you are doing and thinking as you drive along. You may feel odd at first; it probably looks odder still to anyone who sees you talking to yourself, but you will soon become accustomed to it and will then realise its true value.

A typical commentary might sound like this: 'Turning into Green Lane – accelerating in second gear, now moving up to third – make sure the turn signal has been cancelled – careful with the speed, there's a 30mph limit – school warning there, school coming up on the left – it's mid-afternoon and there may be children about – slow down a little, stay in third and be alert – there's a pair of feet under that parked van – could be a child waiting to cross or dash out – give a warning toot on the horn and move well out into the road – check mirror first – now signal – move out – we're past the buildings and into the 40 limit, so the speed goes up – into fourth – check the mirror – there's a parked car ahead right on the approach to that bend, too, and someone is in the driving seat, so maybe it's about to move off – yes, a puff of smoke from the exhaust so he's started the engine – I'll hang back a little – just as well I did – here he comes, pulling out without even a glance in his mirror, let alone a signal – following him through the bend, keeping a little to the right as it's a left-hander and this way I can get maximum vision round the curve'.

At first you will be amazed at how much of this kind of detailed observation and planning you are leaving out. But with a little practice you will be pleasantly surprised at how much you are putting in. At one time, a five-minute session of this kind of commentary driving formed part of the advanced test, but it was later omitted since the Institute felt that those inexperienced in it might feel that they couldn't do themselves justice. But advanced motorists attach considerable importance to commentary driving, so it remains a voluntary part of the test which the candidate can include if he wishes.

3

SAFETY AT THE WHEEL

In this chapter, we deal with the correct driving position and the location of the steering wheel in relation to pedals and seat. There is, however, a little more to safety at the wheel than that and these other aspects are worth getting right.

The first essential is the mirrors. You need a good interior mirror that gives a broad field of vision, preferably right up to the blind spots formed by the rear quarter panels between the back window and rear side windows, so that you know exactly what's happening behind you. In Chapter 8 you will read that a convex glass encompasses a wider field of view but unfortunately it has the effect of distorting the image and giving a false impression of distance, and for this reason we prefer a larger area of plain glass. If the interior mirror tends to vibrate, as many do, brace it lightly against the windscreen with a small strut, otherwise the image will be blurred and useless. You will find the main fixing is strong enough to hold the brace in place.

Give careful thought to your choice of exterior mirror, as there is a wide selection available on the market. A pair of wing mirrors will do a lot to open up the otherwise blind spots near the rear sides of the car, but one mounted on the driver's door frame does have the advantage of revealing overtaking vehicles which might otherwise remain unseen. However, as it is much nearer the driver, it does call for more refocusing of the eyes.

Next, safety belts. The choice nowadays is between inertia or static three-point harnesses as simple lap straps are rarely seen. Static belts are cheaper and, because they are fixed, should be fail-safe. There is

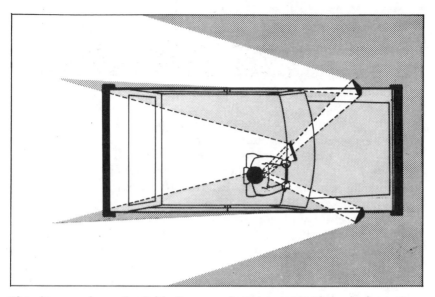

This diagram shows the field of rearward view provided by a good set of mirrors. Always check that they are correctly adjusted in relation to your position at the wheel, or those tantalising blind spots near the rear wings might enlarge sufficiently to hide a cyclist or other hazard. Incidentally, door mirrors are becoming more and more common and have certain advantages over the wing mirrors illustrated here.

no mechanism to go wrong and, as long as the webbing has not frayed or the mounting points rusted through, there is no reason why it should fail to work. Passengers sometimes prefer this type of harness because it holds them more securely against the forces of cornering and braking and the same can even apply to the driver. But not everyone likes being restricted in this way, and for the driver there are still many cars in which you cannot reach some of the minor controls when wearing a static belt. It must be worn tight, otherwise it cannot be expected to do the wearer much good in an accident.

Inertia-reel belts adjust automatically to the user's position and lock only if the inertia of the car changes, such as by a sudden application of the brakes. Most people soon ignore the light pressure it places on them, and appreciate the fact that they can either bend forward, or even turn round in the seat. It is essential, of course, that the self-locking device on the reel remains in perfect working order and that there is nothing on the floor of the car – such as an umbrella

– which could slide across and jam the reel to prevent it keeping the belt tight.

A safety harness is just as desirable in the rear seats although a plain lap strap may be sufficient if the wearer is held far enough away from the front seats.

Young children – usually those under 10 years of age – are too small to wear adult seat belts properly, and should be protected by a British Standards Institution-approved child safety seat. These usually come with a miniature version of a full four-point adult harness for use between about five years, when the child may outgrow its special seat, and around 10, when it is usually big enough to use an adult belt safely.

A young child will not need a head restraint as the seat back performs that function, but for adults a proper purpose-built restraint, designed as an integral part of the seat, can help prevent potentially serious whiplash injuries to the upper vertebrae caused by the head snapping back if a vehicle crashes into the back of your car. To work properly, it is essential for the restraint to be positioned only a few inches from the back of your head (and so, ideally, it should be adjustable) and fixed very securely to the main seat frame.

New cars often have head restraints as a standard fixture or optional extra, and manufacturers make them small enough not to interfere with vision to the rear. These restraints are well worth having if possible, but they may not be on your dealer's normal list of options, either because they are not available for the car you want or because they are offered only on cars to be exported to countries where they are required by law. Remember that 'head rests', sold in accessory shops to clip onto the back of the seat, do no more than the name implies. They are fine as a means for a sleepy passenger to rest his head during a long journey but for this reason they are inadvisable for use by drivers. And as head restraints their attachment to the seat can never be strong enough to be safe.

Basic safety equipment in the car should include a first aid kit, the contents of which should be used only by someone competent (some local authorities offer courses), and a fire extinguisher, which should be of a reputable brand with an adequate supply of the BCF chemical capable of dealing with both petrol and electrical fires.

Finally, always carry out regular checks on tyres (pressure and condition), brakes, steering, lights, windscreen wipers and washers, and other safety-related items listed in your car's instruction manual.

4

A STATE OF MIND

Every adult of sound body and mind has the right to ride or drive some form of independent transport on the public highway in this country, whether he chooses a moped or a Bentley Mulsanne. The tiny minority who would do away with cars for environmental or other reasons seem to ignore the fact that, without private means of transport, the country's public transport system could not begin to cope with our 20,000,000 licence holders and their passengers. Local bus and train fares are often low but it would be much more expensive for a family going on holiday or visiting relatives in a different part of the country to take the train rather than the car.

This is what car travel is all about and long may people have the right and ability to move freely around the country. Having said that, it is clearly essential to have some control over the use of cars to prevent the road system becoming jammed and the accident rate continuing to soar. So while the ownership of a car is a right – controlled by the authorities – the licence to drive it is a privilege and not a right. The licence must be earned by acquiring enough skill and responsibility at the wheel to pass the Government driving test, which is less rigorous than in many other countries. Once obtained, the licence must be kept up by the maintenance of at least a minimum standard of safe and law-abiding driving and, should you fall below that standard, you will be kept off the road, either by a court disqualifying you from holding a licence, or by the insurance companies refusing to give you cover at a price you can afford.

It is therefore important to look at the frame of mind in which driving is best approached. Apprehension is potentially as dangerous as aggression. The driver who hangs back and fails to make a decision when faced with a hazard is equally as likely to cause an accident as the one who drives without care and consideration for other road users.

Enjoy your motoring – the techniques of advanced driving will help you get more pleasure out of your car – but be careful to retain control of your emotions. Beware the spring morning with little traffic about when your joy of life can allow your increase in speed to go unnoticed.

Always be tolerant towards other drivers. Never retaliate, even though aggression by another motorist may send up your pulse rate. It is essential that the bad behaviour or stupidity of others never affect your own manner, so put your own poise and safety before any attempt at retaliation, however hard this may be. Some drivers, intentionally or otherwise, accelerate when being overtaken. This is obviously a dangerous practice, and a number of Continental countries have recognised it as such and made it an offence. There is perhaps a natural instinct which makes us want to stay in front, and so causes the accelerator to be pressed a little harder, and some drivers do it without realising. It means that the overtaking driver is exposed on the wrong side of the road for a longer period of time, and this is potentially hazardous. He may be forced to cut in sharply when he does pass you, or be compelled to cancel the manoeuvre, brake hard, and pull in behind you. In either case, you will be guilty of endangering another road user.

Of course, it is simple enough to advise motorists to retain their dignity and courtesy at all times but there must be times for all of us when outside stresses make this impossible, and when that happens you should not be driving. It is difficult to assess the degree of emotional stress sufficient to make you a risk on the road. You may be too distraught to recognise the symptoms in yourself but bear in mind that after a domestic tiff or a confrontation at work you will not be able to concentrate totally on the considerable responsibility of driving a car safely, for you may be tempted to let off steam by driving aggressively or too quickly. In the same way, speed limits must be observed no matter how late you may be for an appointment.

No one is likely to get behind the wheel while suffering from a severe bout of influenza, but even minor illnesses can seriously affect your driving. A minor cold is likely to slow your reactions and dull your judgement, and may make you bad tempered. When you are feeling under the weather, only you can decide if you are fit enough to drive. If you decide that you are, drive with extra care since you are physically and mentally below par. Doctors always try to warn patients about the side-effects of drugs they prescribe, and if they don't it is your responsibility to ask. Many drugs tend to make you feel sleepy and slow down your reactions, while others may impair your mental or physical faculties in other ways – perhaps without you being fully aware of it. Driving under the influence of drugs may be as risky as driving under the influence of alcohol, and should be out of the question as far as the responsible driver is concerned.

5

STEERING

One of the basic requirements of safe driving is to sit at the wheel properly. Driving becomes unnecessarily tiring if your driving position is wrong, and it will reduce the degree of control you have over the car. It will also reveal your inadequacies as a driver to a trained observer. Probably the most common error is that of sitting too close to the wheel, which usually suggests that the driver lacks confidence in his ability to handle the car. It can also mean poor eyesight. The motorist may not be aware of any defect, but unconsciously compensates for it by placing himself as close to the road as possible.

On the other hand, you can make the mistake of being too relaxed, slouching in the driving seat with your right arm on the window-sill and the hand off the wheel. Left-handed steering – perhaps with the hand casually holding a spoke of the wheel – points to overconfidence, almost to the point of boredom. Sloppy driving can develop unconsciously, and even people who try to drive properly have been known to complain that the door pull on a new car was too low for comfortable use as an arm rest.

Then there is the 'boy racer' brigade. They seek to emulate their racing driver heroes who recline in the cockpits of their cars with arms seemingly stretched to a tiny steering wheel. These would-be racers try to copy the position in their modest saloons but learn to their cost that procedures which are ideal on the racing circuit are to be avoided on the road. A racing driver has to lie back to avoid sticking up into the air stream from his low-slung car, and the steering wheel has to be small because the steering itself is high geared and just a twitch of the wrist is enough to set the car on the right line through the corners. The straight-arm technique is dictated by this sensitive steering and the lack of space in the narrow cockpit.

This technique is not only irrevelant to road driving, but also reduces the driver's control and is as tiring as sitting hunched over the wheel.

Now we have dealt with the wrong driving positions, let us turn our attention to the right one. It should allow your hands to fall naturally into either a 'ten-to-two' or 'quarter-to-three' position on the steering wheel while keeping the arms bent at the elbow through an angle of 90 degrees or more. Make sure your legs are positioned comfortably in relation to the pedals: they should not be splayed out around the steering wheel, nor should you be sitting so far away that you have to stretch to depress the clutch pedal to the floor. Drivers do not have the same leg and trunk length proportionate to arm length, so this position is not easy to arrange. While manufacturers try to make cars with a range of adjustment likely to suit the majority of customers, it is difficult to suit every motorist. Most cars, apart from really cheap versions, now have a seat back that adjusts for rake, which greatly assists the chances of obtaining a good driving position. If your car lacks this, however, you can buy a rake-adjustable seat from an accessory shop or, if you want to get nearer the wheel, you can fit a supplementary back rest. These should fix firmly in place, and offer the bonus of a better lumbar posture which can ease back troubles. Never use a loose cushion for this job. Once your driving position is right, you will find that the car becomes easier, more enjoyable and less wearing to drive.

With your hands correctly positioned as outlined above, and spaced equidistant on the upper part of the rim, you are best placed to make a sudden yet accurate and controlled movement of the steering should a violent swerve be demanded. It is hard to imagine how a man with both hands positioned at '12 o'clock', or with just one hand limply at '6 o'clock', copes with such an emergency.

Normal steering movements should be made by feeding the wheel through your hands. For example, when turning right, pull the rim down a few inches with the right hand and let it slide through the fingers of the left. As your right hand reaches the bottom of the natural arc keep up the turning movement by bringing the left hand, now gripping the rim, upwards. At the same time move your right hand up ready to repeat the operation. It needs only a little practice to develop this technique into a neat, controlled movement that applies steering lock smoothly and progressively, while retaining a firm grip on the wheel at all times. It is surprising how many people manage to let go of the wheel completely for long moments during

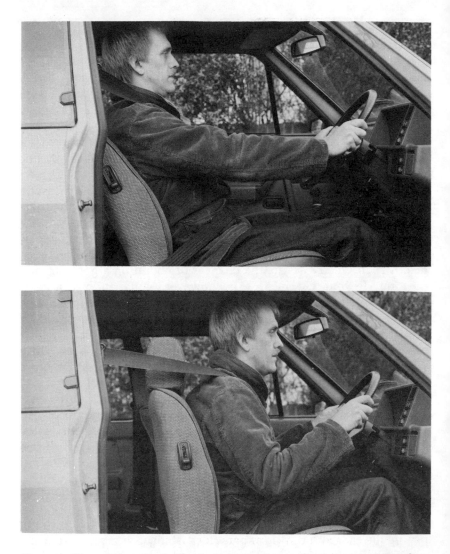

Your position at the wheel. The *top* picture shows the 'boy racer' straight arm technique – fine for the narrow confines of a racing car cockpit, but totally unsuitable for a road car. The picture *below* illustrates one of the most common bad driving positions: sitting too close to the wheel. This often reflects a lack of confidence and may be a pointer to short-sightedness. The correct position is shown in the *above, right* picture. The arms and legs are comfortably positioned, with the hands falling naturally at the 'ten-to-two' or 'quarter-to-three' position.

their normal driving – and yet do not realise it. As you come out of the turn straighten up by reversing the method. Neither hand should ever be allowed to stray past the '12 o'clock' position. If it does, the degree of fine control you have over the steering is substantially reduced. Even at the apex of the tightest turn, your hands should be opposite each other, ready to apply correct lock should a skid start, or to bring in more lock should it be needed.

As you come out of a bend there is a strong temptation to allow the self-centring action of the steering to pull the wheel back to the ahead position as you allow the rim to slip through your fingers. This method is widely favoured but it has the serious disadvantage that, if sudden steering movement is called for, you have to waste valuable fractions of a second getting a grip on the wheel and then orientating yourself as to just where the front wheels are pointing in relation to the steering. Only during low speed manoeuvring, when turning the car around in a car park, for instance, can this method be considered advisable. At such a time it is also acceptable – although hardly necessary – to take one or both hands past '12 o'clock' on the wheel rim when turning.

The crossed-hands technique should be avoided at all other times, simply because your hands are not well placed to steer the car while in this position. It is quite different for racing drivers; on the track speed is of primary importance, there is room to make mistakes and danger is a secondary consideration. None of these aspects apply on the public road.

Many motorists imagine their car is three feet wider than it really is because they do not take the trouble to judge it accurately. Once you have a precise idea of your car's width and length, you will be able to negotiate a path through congested traffic more easily, or to get into a tight parking spot which previously looked too small. Find an empty car park on a Sunday morning and use markers to practise accurate steering and to get to know the exact width of your car. Once this art is perfected, it is important not to use it to overtake vehicles too closely as it could startle other drivers and cause them to swerve.

It should not be forgotten that, in addition to positioning the hands correctly, the wheel must be held in the right way as well. Inexperienced or timid drivers have a tendency to grip the wheel too tightly which is tiring. It also tends to make steering movements coarser, and when cruising on the motorway at 70mph it may make the car wander from side to side. Cars have a built-in tendency to run straight, but to do so they respond best to a light but firm hold on the wheel. A really tight grip is transmitted down to the front wheels, making them over-react to every bump in the road. A gentle hand is especially important with rear-engined cars if they are not to be influenced by cross winds on exposed roads and motorways. It is rather like horse riding: keep a firm but gentle hold on the reins. Perspiration can make plastic or wooden steering wheel rims dangerously slippery, causing the driver to grip the wheel even more tightly. The answer is a lace-on leather cover for the wheel, or driving gloves thin enough to permit a sensitive grip.

Thick gauntlets should not be used for driving in the winter. They are clumsy, and tend to make your steering coarse, which in bad conditions might lead to a skid. Since modern car heaters are so effective anyway, heavy gloves are unnecessary.

Sensitivity in steering is of paramount importance, especially if your car is one of the growing number equipped with power-assisted steering, which is designed to take the drudgery out of the job. In principle, there is nothing wrong with power steering since it does make driving big, heavy cars far more pleasant, but it does rob you of some of that all-important 'feel' that comes up through the wheel rim to tell you how the front wheels are reacting to the road surface. An experienced driver gets a lot of useful information in this way with normal steering and the better power-assisted varieties. But some power systems lack this characteristic and it is essential to treat them with consideration. On a wet road, a sudden steering movement can cause the tyres' road grip to break free and start a front-wheel skid. Treat power-assistance with respect, and take care not to abuse its artificial lightness.

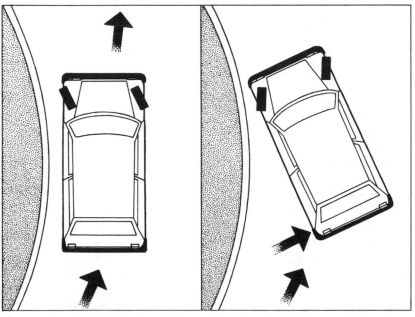

The position of a car's front wheels in an understeer situation (*left*) and an oversteer situation (*right*).

We cannot end this chapter without discussing the much-quoted – and frequently misunderstood – terms 'oversteer' and 'understeer'. They do not, as many people seem to think, have anything to do with any action taken by the driver, but refer to the basic handling characteristics of the car. Most cars, especially those with front-wheel drive, tend to understeer, which simply means they need more steering lock than might be expected in order to hold them into a bend. Others, and particularly rear-engined models, need *less* and you may find yourself having to ease off the steering a little to keep the car on the correct course. This is oversteer. So the 'under' and 'over' refer to how the car responds to being deflected from the straight and narrow by the steering.

6

BRAKING

Braking is an integral part of advanced driving and its proper implementation is rather more involved than simply pressing the brake pedal when you want to slow down or stop. Before looking at braking in detail, we should first dispel some of the myths which surround it.

First, disc brakes are not intrinsically more powerful than the old-fashioned drum type, so the few people who still drive around with a 'discs' sign stuck on their boot lid are impressing no one. It is resistance to fade which makes the disc brake superior. A brake of any kind heats when it is used and, when it is applied frequently and with a lot of pressure, the temperature will reach a point at which braking power is diminished and finally disappears altogether. This is called brake fade. It is possible to drive for a lifetime without experiencing this phenomenon but it can arise at the least welcome moment, such as when you are descending a mountain pass with hairpin bends every few hundred yards. The warning sign comes when you find it is necessary to apply extra pressure on the brake pedal to achieve the same stopping power, and as the heat builds up you will find the car hardly responding to the brakes at all. The only answer is to stop at the first sign of fade and give the overheated surfaces time to cool down.

The disadvantage of the drum brake is that it is not as good at dispersing the heat and starts to fade earlier. But brake fade is rarely experienced these days, mainly because disc brakes are so widely used. But either type of brake – disc or drum – is quite powerful enough to lock up a wheel if you hit the pedal hard enough, even on a dry road. The effectiveness of a car's brakes is limited by the tyres' grip on the road. A set of four modern tyres does a pretty remarkable job by keeping a car weighing a ton or two on the road when each

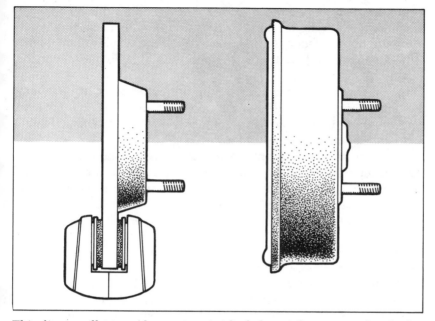

This diagram illustrates how more air (shaded area) flows over a disc brake (*left*) than over a drum brake. It is the cooling effect of this air which makes discs less prone to 'brake fade'.

tyre's contact area of tread rubber on the road surface is little more than the size of a man's shoe sole.

Even the best tyres can be pushed beyond the limit, of course, and they will begin to lose their grip, lock up and start skidding if the brake pedal is hit too hard, and the road surface is wet. In a skid with locked wheels the car is not slowing at anything like the best possible rate, and to the driver it even seems to accelerate. The most powerful braking comes when the wheels are still rotating just before the moment when the brake pressure locks them up. It is worth recognising this moment in your own car but unwise to try to find it by practising on a public road. The best place is on a skid pan, disused airfield or a large, empty car park. Alternatively, the local authority Road Safety Officer may know of somewhere suitable. Practise emergency stops at progressively higher speeds as this experience will be invaluable when a real emergency happens.

The dab technique is one way to keep the wheels rolling for

optimum braking in a crash stop. The driver does this by applying the brakes in a series of short, sharp stabs rather than exerting steady pressure on the pedal. Each stab may lock the wheels momentarily but as you ease off ready for the next push they will start rotating again. This method is best kept for wet or icy roads where wheel lock starts easily. Some car manufacturers now offer automatic anti-skid systems which work in much the same way by using speed sensors and pressure limiting valves, all controlled by a computer, to do the work of the human brain and foot.

The experts in this technique are rally drivers who use what they call 'cadence' braking, in which the hard pushes on the brake pedal are timed to coincide with the spring frequency of the front suspension. This means they are taking advantage of the nose-dive characteristic exhibited by most cars under heavy braking. Deceleration puts an extra load on the front of the car, which pushes it down on its springs and so increases the weight on the front tyres. As the front tyres do most of the work under braking, their grip is usefully – if momentarily – improved. When the brake is released the front of the car lifts for a moment, then bounces down again under the action of the springs. As that happens, the pedal is pushed hard again and the front tyres grip better as a result of the extra weight on them, and are therefore less likely to lock and start a skid. It is possible, with practice, to time the pedal movements to coincide perfectly with the car's nose-dive action.

This technique is a highly specialised one, suitable only for use in dire emergency and calling for plenty of private practice. With foresight, skill and some luck, you will never need it. The essential thing to remember is that brakes stop the wheels, but tyres stop the car. Nevertheless, it is vitally important to know your car's braking capabilities and to recognise the limits of adhesion between even the best tyres and the road surface.

Just as important is an understanding of the distances needed to stop a car. You need much more room than many motorists realise, even in good conditions: a fact borne out by the multiple nose-to-tail accidents which occur on motorways. The distance required to stop does not increase in direct proportion to speed, and the old rule about 'one car's length for every 10mph' is only part of the picture. A mere 90 feet at 60mph, which this misconception suggests, gives room enough if the car in front simply slows down, but you have to bear in mind it may stop a good deal quicker, perhaps by hitting a vehicle ahead. If this should happen, you need at least twice as much space between you to pull up. The 'one car's length per 10mph' represents thinking distance only.

The advanced motorist will learn to estimate safe braking distances automatically, but if in doubt there is a useful rule of thumb formula: square the speed and divide by 20 to get the distance in feet. For 60mph, therefore, $60 \times 60 = 3600 \div 20 = 180$ feet. As you will see, this is exactly twice what that old rule suggests. Braking distances rise disproportionately quickly, so at 60mph you will need four times the space required at 30mph. And to this figure must be added the thinking distance. It must be borne in mind that these figures are for a good car on a reasonable road surface. Add rain or, worse still, a slippery film of water, oil, rubber, or dust that often coats summer roads, or snow and ice, and the figures rise alarmingly. A driver travelling at 60mph on snow and ice – should anyone other than a rally driver be so foolish – might find himself needing a third of a mile to stop, and even with that summer sludge the figure could still be around 750 feet.

The thinking distance must never be forgotten, as it has to be added to the braking distance. Even people with the sharpest reactions need time for their eye to perceive that there is a hazard ahead, for the message to be flashed to the brain, for the brain to decide that braking is required, and to get this order down to the foot which must then move from the accelerator pedal to the brake and start applying pressure. All that may take only 0·5 seconds – and you need remarkably rapid reactions to achieve that figure – but in that time a car travelling at 30mph will have moved 22 feet closer to the hazard. Go back to the example of 60mph and the thinking distance becomes 44 feet or, for most drivers, something more like 60–80 feet. That is a significant figure to be added to the actual *braking* distance.

From this you will see that the old saying 'I stopped dead' can never apply, even from a speed as low as 10mph. Anyone who has acquired the skills of advanced motoring will find that it is seldom necessary to brake fiercely in normal driving. Quite apart from the adverse effects on your passengers and any other considerations, it wears out the brakes and tyres much more quickly. You should apply the brakes smoothly and progressively for about two-thirds or three-quarters of the distance in which you wish to stop, easing up on the pressure for the last section. Should you have miscalculated, or find that you need to stop that much sooner than expected – the man ahead may pull up short of the Stop line, for instance – you are left with a reserve.

A driver who keeps the brakes on quite hard until the car stops jolts his passengers, although he will probably not even notice it himself. To prevent this, literally, sickening jolt, ease off the pressure and then for the last few feet ease back still further so that the car rolls to a halt under the lightest touch on the pedal. With practice the moment of stopping can be imperceptible: an art perfected by chauffeurs. A glance out of the corner of the eye which shows the passenger's head not even nodding forward will let you know when you have achieved this. Cost is another good reason to avoid harsh braking, even when travelling alone. Locking the wheels and slithering to a halt from only 30mph can wipe two normal months' wear off the tyres.

Brake failure is rare these days, and made all the more so as a result of the duplication of operating systems on many cars. But it has still not been eliminated altogether. Discs have done much to get rid of the fade problem, of course, but they can still get wet since – unlike the drum type – they are exposed to the elements. This problem is prevented on most cars by splash guards, but even these do not always stop water building up on the disc during, for instance, a long motorway drive through a rainstorm. If it has not been necessary to brake for many miles in these conditions, it is possible you may find a film of water has built up between disc and friction pad. Zero retardation follows, usually only for a few seconds while the 'lubricant' is wiped away by the pad, but it can feel like an eternity if you have inadvertently left braking to the last minute. The answer is to dab the pedal lightly once every few miles. If the car is prone to this fault, that should be enough to wipe away the water.

Real and total brake failure is another matter. If the cause is a slow leak of hydraulic fluid, you may get some warning: the pedal will travel further than normal and may feel spongy. There will be a temporary response if you pump hard and bring more fluid into the system from the reservoir, but the cure must be an immediate location and rectification of the underlying cause. Unless you are fairly highly skilled, that is best left to a garage. The most alarming type of brake failure is when you have no warning. The first indication you are given is when the brake pedal sags uselessly on the floor. If this happens, use the hand brake, as this has a separate and mechanical – as opposed to hydraulic – linkage, and slow the car by dropping down through the gears without revving up as you engage the lower gear ratios. You may still be able to steer out of trouble. Most drivers manage to go through life without ever experiencing this rather frightening phenomenon, but at least you know what to do should such an emergency arise.

On the other hand, the cardinal sin of braking on bends is something that most drivers do most of the time. And it is only because of the excellent handling qualities of most modern cars that their drivers get away with it without incident. All braking should be carried out with the car running in a straight line, except when travelling slowly. It is easy to cause a skid by braking on a bend when driving at all quickly, especially if the road is wet. This happens because the centrifugal force makes the body roll towards the outside of the curve. This takes the weight off the inside wheels and that in turn makes them a good deal more prone to locking up and precipitating a skid. And that is not the end of the matter. There is a limit to the amount of adhesive ability of any tyre, whether it is transmitting power from the engine, steering the car, or keeping it on the chosen path (and thereby resisting centrifugal force) around a curve. If 80 per cent of that power is being used for steering around the curve and the driver asks for a further 40 per cent of total adhesive power by braking suddenly, he is calling for 120 per cent of the tyre's adhesive capacity. Obviously something's got to give, and the result will be a skid. Modern tyre and suspension design allows drivers to get away with a lot when braking while cornering, but it is still possible to go too far and finish up at best frightened, at worst in a crash.

Motorists with automatic transmission in their car sometimes prefer to operate the brakes with their left foot which is otherwise redundant. There seems little point in this as a driver hardly wants to be braking and accelerating at the same time. There is always a danger that in an emergency the driver's mind will react instinctively and send the right foot across to press on a pedal that is already being operated by the consciously trained left foot. The result is that you brake with both feet, lock up the wheels and get into a skid.

Racing drivers 'heel and toe' when changing down through the gears as they approach a corner on the track. Some drivers favour this technique on the road but with little point. You may save a few fractions of a second which are important on the race track but should mean nothing on the public highway, and there is always the chance you may not brake properly as you are trying to operate two pedals at the same moment with one foot. The term 'heel and toe' is rather misleading anyway. What actually happens is that the sole of the foot presses the brake while the side of the foot – or the heel, if the pedals are so positioned – is depressing the accelerator to rev up the engine for the next downward change. A clever technique, but one with little relevance to everyday driving and one which, incidentally, wears out the sides of your shoes.

Finally, in this discussion on braking, there is the matter of keeping an eye on the people around you. Watch out for the driver in front who pulls up sharply. Allow for an even greater braking distance between your car and his as insurance against his miscalculating. Look out for the crumpled old banger looming up in your rearview mirror, and ask yourself whether his brakes are likely to be in first-class condition. And beware the car which 'rides' your back bumper. Try to give these drivers extra warning that they will have to slow down by braking earlier than usual, starting with a touch on the pedal to bring on your brake lights. Even better, leave yourself more braking distance than usual so that the space can be used to provide the driver behind with more stopping distance.

7

ACCELERATION AND ECONOMY

Like so many other aspects of advanced motoring, there is a great deal more to using a car's power than meets the eye. While we would not suggest that a car should be driven hard, or its performance abused, power used in the right place and at the right time can be a useful aid to safety. It is often better to accelerate out of harm's way when confronted by a hazard than to brake or steer round it. It is surprising how rarely this technique is used when you bear in mind the efforts of engineers to provide adequate performance, and how much attention people pay to this when choosing a car. It is probably true that few cars are driven to the full extent of their potential but moments do arise, such as when overtaking, when more force with the right foot could keep a driver out of trouble, rather than getting him into it.

When you decide to overtake, you will have to move over to the 'wrong' side of the road unless you are on a motorway or dual carriageway. The longer you are there, the longer you are exposed to the possibility of coming into contact with traffic coming from the opposite direction. If you have overestimated your own car's over-taking potential, you will need all the time you can get to pass by. So the first requirement is to find out the capabilities of your car. It is wise to find a deserted stretch of open road with no low speed limits and put your car through its paces. The manufacturer's handbook will advise you on the maximum speed in any gear. Try it a couple of times, if only to prove to yourself that the car can take it. You will probably be surprised at just how much acceleration is available, even from a modest car, and it will give you a clear idea of what you can expect in an emergency.

Normally when overtaking you will not need to venture to such extremes but you should still get by as quickly as seems reasonable, from both your own point of view and that of the overtaken driver.

Remember to select the correct gear before starting to overtake — although third is usually the right one, second may be better (many cars can exceed 60mph in this gear). As you start the manoeuvre, let the power come in smoothly; opening the throttle sharply is unnecessary and, on a slippery road or greasy city street, could just break the driving wheels' traction and start the wheelspin that leads to a skid. It should be possible to complete the entire manoeuvre without changing up until you have returned safely to the left of the road. But if you do have to change up early, do so quickly but smoothly as a violent clutch action can have just the same effect as too quick a depression of the accelerator.

Every driver needs what is called acceleration sense, which is the ability to judge, almost without thinking, whether you can safely carry out a manoeuvre and, having decided that you can, to make full use of the performance while still driving safely. This comes from experience of the car you are driving. A fine ability to control the accelerator is required to produce good acceleration sense. It is an excellent idea to keep a pair of thin-soled shoes in the car just for driving, since your touch on the accelerator should be very delicate.

Since fuel economy is of such importance to most drivers, it is worth remembering that a significant amount of petrol can be saved if you avoid the pointless habit of revving up the engine with the gearbox in neutral, as it achieves absolutely nothing at all. Increased skill in the correct use of the accelerator will do a good deal to save fuel. Ramming the accelerator down to the floor, revving too high and driving impatiently all use up costly petrol.

If the conditions are bad enough, such behaviour can be the cause of an accident. Nowadays even quite ordinary cars have more than adequate power to spin the wheels if the road is wet enough. Even getting away from traffic lights can set the wheels spinning, if an over-brisk engagement of the clutch is combined with heavy pressure on the accelerator, though this is more a possibility than a probability. A car with front-wheel-drive will probably react by shuddering and producing lots of engine noise with little forward movement. More seriously, the same mistake in a car with power to the back wheels can result in the rear end sliding round in a slow-motion rear-end skid that must be corrected with opposite lock steering. Whether your car has power to the front or rear wheels, the answer is simply to take your foot off the accelerator pedal and then reapply it more delicately.

It would be wrong to conclude this chapter on acceleration without making the following point. After a cold start in the morning, your car may not respond properly to the demands of acceleration for the first few miles of motoring. Until it warms up, a sudden opening of the throttle may leave it gasping for breath and in an extreme case can even cause it to stall. The situation is often made worse if the car has a manual choke which is not at the right setting. Therefore it is important to operate the accelerator progressively, and to avoid demanding more from the engine than it is capable of giving. Do not try to warm up the engine by revving it when the car is stationary unless the manufacturer's handbook specifically advises this. The running temperature will be reached much more quickly when driving on the road.

8

OBSERVATION

Skilled observation can keep you out of trouble in 90 per cent of all potentially dangerous incidents. It demands practice and thought but it enables you to read the road ahead in much the same way as a ship's master reads his chart in difficult waters. You have to learn to absorb a vast amount of information from what at first appears to be irrelevant detail: something all drivers do to a certain extent. But the real value of skilled observation – as with other aspects of advanced driving – does not come until it has been developed into an art.

The first essential is to make sure that your own vision is satisfactory. A worrying number of drivers have eyesight defects of varying degrees of seriousness and, what's more, many are totally unaware that anything is wrong. A person who read a number plate without difficulty when passing his test 20 years ago may now be suffering from a potentially lethal fault in his vision without realising it, because eyesight usually deteriorates slowly. Over the years the fault may develop unnoticed, possibly with the sufferer subconsciously compensating for it. The 25-yard number plate test is not demanding enough. Even with little or no sight in one eye it is possible to pass it without difficulty, although it will probably mean that judgement of distance is poor – obviously dangerous in the extreme. The test also fails to diagnose tunnel vision, which is the tendency to concentrate only on the view directly in front and to exclude anything more than a few degrees outside. This is a serious matter as good peripheral sight is necessary if you are to be aware of what is happening on each side of the car. You might also be long- or short-sighted and sight trouble of this kind is often proportionately worse at night.

Another serious eye defect is colour blindness, particularly when it takes the form of an inability to identify red, as this is the colour used for all danger signs on the road, as well as brake lights and traffic lights. It is worth going to an optician for a proper check on your eyesight. There will probably be nothing wrong but, if there is, it is much better to find out now rather than after a serious accident when someone finds you are to blame as a result of your defective sight.

It is an offence not to wear glasses which you do in fact need for driving. Always keep a pair of dark glasses in the car, not only in the summer but also in the winter, when the sun setting low on the horizon can be brilliant. Economy here is pointless, as it is with anything connected with road safety. Sunglasses with cheap plastic lenses scratch easily and blot out too much of your perception in shaded areas. Polarised glasses are among the best, but try them in your car first as distracting stress patterns can sometimes be seen in toughened glass windscreens when this type of lens is used. The ideal is a pair of high quality, lightly tinted glass lenses, but they can be costly. These can be supplied as prescription lenses, as well. Avoid special night driving glasses. These normally have yellow lenses or no glass at all, but an arrangement of slats or blinkers presumably intended to shield the wearer's eyes. Such glasses can be dangerous.

While a decent pair of dark glasses are useful during the day and can help considerably to reduce eyestrain, they should never be used at night. It is easy to understand why many motorists do this, but they are giving away an important part of their vision. In the same way that sunglasses reduce the glare from oncoming headlights, they also reduce the amount of light reaching the eyes from all other sources such as marginally lit areas like the nearside kerb which fall outside the headlamp beam. This could mean that you fail to see something – or someone – possibly with fatal results.

There is no point in putting your eyes under a serious strain if they are functioning properly (if they aren't, then you should not be driving anyway). Headlights on approaching cars can be dazzling, but the answer is to avoid looking at them. With a little willpower, you can train yourself to look away from them and look towards the nearside of the road instead. This ability will come naturally in time and eventually you will begin to appreciate the oncoming light for the way it throws a little light into your path. While you are contending with the lights on passing traffic, it is inevitable that you will concentrate your gaze on the road immediately ahead. However, one must look further ahead at all other times, day or night. It is a

The importance of good eyesight. The *top, left* picture shows the view
from behind the wheel of a person with average eyesight. Everything is
clear, and peripheral vision is adequate. The *centre, left* picture shows the
effect of long-sightedness, with the foreground blurred and the distant
objects in focus. Short-sightedness is even worse, as is illustrated by the
bottom, left picture. Everything ahead of you is dangerously blurred.
Tunnel vision (*top*) is a less common defect, but potentially disastrous.
The view straight ahead is fine, but peripheral vision is badly affected. The
hazards of such a defect need no elaboration. Finally, some people suffer
from double vision, which can greatly affect your judgement on the road. If
you suffer from these or other defects, it is in your own interest, as well as
that of all other road users, to do something about it.

good idea to try to concentrate your vision on a point some way ahead, while at the same time taking in events even further in the distance, closer to you and on either side. This selective vision will come only with practice but it is well worth training yourself to keep an eye open over as wide a field of vision as possible. An experienced driver with excellent peripheral vision can often point out sights at the side of the road, such as a horse on a hill, that even his passengers have missed, yet at the same time keeping the centre of his gaze focused on the road ahead. The centre of that focus will have to be adjusted as speed increases or decreases, in the same way that a soldier firing a rifle raises or lowers his sights to compensate for the range.

Now we have dealt with direct vision ahead and to the sides, we must turn our attention to the view astern. The interior mirror is essential, but it is not enough to rely on that alone. A pair of wing mirrors is most valuable, as is one mounted on the door frame. Carefully positioned, a full set of mirrors will give you a fine field of vision behind. This can be artificially extended by choosing mirrors with convex glass, but remember that these distort the image and make it more difficult to judge distance. Once you have driven with one of these mirrors, you will realise how tricky it is to know whether the car behind is following at a safe distance, or about to nudge your bumper.

Flat glass is preferable for this reason. There will still be one or two blind spots, whichever sort of glass you choose, notably just above your right shoulder and possibly at the three-quarter rear position on either side, particularly if the car is a coupé with 'blind' metal panels at these points. Sadly, there is no simple answer to these blind spots other than always allowing for them when checking your mirrors. The only way to ensure that there is not a car or motorcycle hidden in a blind spot and about to overtake is to ignore the mirror and cast a quick (and we do mean quick) glance over your shoulder if all looks safe ahead. In addition, there is nothing like having a look yourself when moving off or reversing. Never perform the latter manoeuvre until you are quite certain that the road is clear. If your car gives poor vision to the rear, then get out first, walk around and see for yourself. To back blindly, hoping that nothing or no one – a playing child, for instance – is in the way is unforgivable.

Your observation should become more selective on the road. There is a host of visual information and the skill lies in distinguishing that which should be acted upon and that which can be ignored. These are some of the pointers to be noticed:

● Changing road surface (a sudden switch from a dull surface to a shiny one could mean that tyre grip will be reduced and stopping distances lengthened accordingly).

● Building site entrances, farm exits and other points where vehicles can track mud onto the road and make it slippery.

● A bend ahead, often indicated by an abrupt change in direction of the telephone poles (though remember that this cannot be taken as a totally accurate indication since the pole route does sometimes veer away from the road).

● A gap between buildings or trees, which on a windy day can greatly alter the sidewind pressure on your car and cause it to yaw across the road if the driver is caught unawares.

● Unexpected movements by parked vehicles. The parked car with a driver at the wheel might suddenly come out into your path if the driver sets off without thinking. There is also a chance that he or a passenger might swing open a door and climb out into your path.

● Give tradesmen's stationary vans a wide berth on country roads in case the driver gets out on the offside.

● It's no bad idea to glance underneath any parked vehicle for a pair of tell-tale feet about to propel their owner out into the traffic. High risk vehicles in this category include school buses and ice-cream vans.

● Anyone walking along the roadside needs to be watched carefully. Children playing on the pavement often dash into the road without stopping to think or look, and an old person, perhaps with failing sight or hearing, also warrants special attention. Stay on your guard in wet weather, when people often keep their heads down which restricts their line of vision, and are inclined not to do their normal kerb drill because they are perhaps hurrying for shelter.

● At all times, cyclists need special attention. They are greatly influenced by wind and rain, and are often unskilled on their machines, so do give them a wide berth. It has been ruled in the High Court that a cyclist is 'entitled to his wobble', so if you pass one too closely it will put you at risk from a legal standpoint, quite apart from the risk to which you may subject the cyclist.

● Good observation of other vehicles will give you plenty of information. A puff of smoke from the exhaust of a lorry on a steep hill will tell you that the driver has changed down, and is likely to travel even more slowly. A van or car with battered bodywork is clearly more likely to be involved in an accident and should be avoided. Those drivers who slouch at the wheel, steer with one hand and appear to be holding on the roof with the other are likewise best avoided. If you are behind a bus, watch out for a passenger putting his hand up to the bell, which will give you advance warning that the bus is likely to stop.

In Britain, we are lucky enough to have a fairly adequate system of road signs. No driver, however experienced, will fail to benefit from referring to the *Highway Code*, and memorising the different basic shapes that indicate the warning signs (a triangle), the advisory ones (a rectangle) and the mandatory ones (a circle). You should in time know all the individual signs by heart, so that just a glance will be enough to tell you what to expect.

You will develop your own methods as your observation skill increases. For instance, it is possible to overcome the blind spots at staggered T-junctions, where visibility down the approach road is limited, by looking into the neighbouring shop windows. Though not totally reliable, they can sometimes act as useful mirrors to give you an idea of what otherwise-invisible traffic is approaching.

9

BENDS AND CORNERS

If a driver goes off the road on a bend, he has no one and nothing else to blame but himself, and if it happens when he is overtaking, there is no room at all for any excuse. Many accidents involving one or two cars happen on bends and it is remarkable that the driver normally does not regard himself at fault. He will probably cite contributory factors such as the road being greasy, or the curve tightening up unexpectedly or adverse camber being encountered as the reasons for the accident. These can, of course, be factors in an accident but they can never be the cause. The reason for going off the road can always be traced back to bad driving in one form or another.

First we must understand what happens to a car when it is steered away from a straight line. Momentum is pulling it forward and there is a natural tendency not to deviate from this straight path, in the same way that a well struck golf ball flies straight and true down the fairway instead of deviating from side to side. To negotiate a car around a corner we turn the steering wheel, which moves the front wheels at an angle to the straight path they are following. The car follows the path dictated by the front wheels, and starts to turn into the curve. At this moment another factor emerges. Centrifugal force tries to push the car outwards in the same way that a string with a weight on the end will tauten if you whirl it around, because the weight is trying to fly outwards under centrifugal force. You feel this force inside the car as it pushes you across the seat, away from the inside of the bend, and if the car has soft suspension it will react by rolling outwards too.

At this point the tyres have begun to work hard. They are following the curved path you have steered the car into, with one pair probably transmitting some power to the road while at the same time resisting the centrifugal forces that try to push the entire car off the road. This is the moment when a driver, if he asks too much of his tyres in these

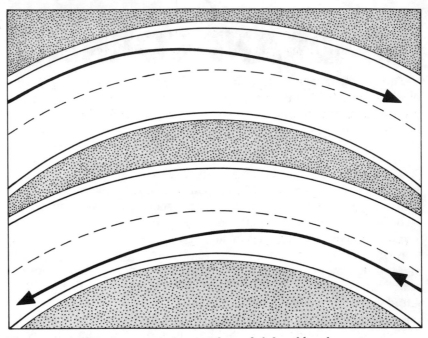

The optimum line for negotiating a right- or left-hand bend on a two-way road. 'Straightening' the curve in this way removes some of the danger from bends in roads, but should not be attempted if it involves changing lanes with other traffic nearby – and don't cross the central line unless you are quite certain that there is no car coming the other way.

conditions, finds they literally lose their grip, a skid starts and there is every chance that the car will run off the road.

Take the bend smoothly, as this is part of the art of cornering well without putting too much stress on the tyres. And there is another important factor to remember: never cut across the inside of a bend to try to achieve the above, as this could inconvenience or even endanger another road user. However, it is still possible to 'straighten out' a bend at least in some measure to improve your own negotiation of it, and your view of it, without hampering anyone else. This phrase 'straighten out' is borrowed from the jargon of racing drivers but it should not be taken as suggesting that there is any virtue in dashing through bends. There is none. Procedures which are acceptable on the race track, with all the cars going in the same direction and able to use the full width of the track, are not to be repeated on the road. It is perfectly permissible, however, to use plenty of your own carriageway to ease the curve and to improve your view around it.

You get the best line through a right-hand bend by entering it well over to the left of your lane, then moving over a little towards the middle, so that your offside wheels are near the central white line as you pass the apex. This provides you with the widest possible arc, reduces the centrifugal force on the tyres and provides the earliest and widest view of the exit. But this amount of 'straightening' should be used only when there is little or no traffic about. With another driver close behind you, it is better to keep to a more regular line, in case he should do something as stupid as trying to overtake you on the curve.

Generalisations about detailed procedure on bends are not really possible, but this should be your basic programme for right-hand ones:

● As you approach the bend, judge the speed at which it can be taken and carry out any braking necessary to get down to that speed while still travelling in a straight line.

● Still in a straight line, change down if it seems necessary to get the right gear to have acceleration on tap as you leave the bend.

● Check the mirror on the approach, in case someone is coming up behind, possibly even contemplating nipping by at – or even before, for some are foolish enough – the exit.

● Remember the racing drivers' adage: 'In slow, out fast', although on the road there should not be too much emphasis placed on the 'fast'.

● Start steering into the curve, bearing in mind how much better it is to make the steering movements smoothly rather than to jerk the car into the turn with a vicious tug at the wheel.

● Depress the accelerator a little as the car responds to the steering. Any car will respond better under power, rather than a trailing throttle, providing it is not overdone, so gentle acceleration will steady it up.

● Check that the exit is clear by looking towards and past the apex. (We will assume that you have not, at this or any other time, got into a situation in which you are driving beyond the car's braking distance, i.e. that you can pull up within the distance you can see to be clear ahead.)

● Push your foot down harder so as to accelerate smoothly out of the bend as you clear the apex. Do not, however, overload the tyres with too much power as this can cause a slide, especially if the roads are wet. And remember that the extra power will usually cause the car to run a little wide, imperceptibly perhaps, but you may still have to make a minor correction by paying off a degree or two of the steering.

Earlier, we described how to make the most of a right-hand bend when conditions allow. On a left-hander, the opposite applies. Make your approach more towards the middle of the road, but still on the correct side of the central line. Move in towards the nearside gutter at the apex, then ease out a little towards your correct position at the exit, a few feet out from the verge.

Braking on a bend is to be avoided if at all possible, but if you have overestimated the safe speed, or if a pedestrian steps out in front of you, you may have little option. You must apply the brakes as lightly as possible, because if you ask too much of the tyres you will lock up the wheels in a skid and skate off the road. If there is room, try to straighten the steering the moment before you brake, then turn again as you take your foot off the brake pedal.

The advanced driver should seldom need it, but emergency braking may occasionally be necessary. He will have looked carefully at the road ahead as he approaches the curve and as he drives through it, and in this way will have been warned of any pedestrians or other road users likely to stray towards his path. A safe speed should have been correctly estimated, according to the conditions, and remembering that it is much better to arrive at a corner travelling too slowly than too quickly. He will also have taken into account the fact that the curve might tighten up as he passes the apex, or might even lead directly into another bend. A conservative speed, correctly judged, at the point of entry will have taken into account such possibilities as these.

The 'unexpected' is quite likely to be around the corner on a country road, whether it is another bend, a wandering animal, or a tractor blocking the road. As in all aspects of advanced driving, the motto here must be to handle the car in accordance with the known and possibly prevailing conditions. It's unlikely, of course, but you might find yourself confronted with another motorist having an accident on a bend. Remember that, if an approaching car starts to skid, you should try to steer away from it rather than braking. The latter course will in all probability leave you well placed to be struck by the other vehicle, but steering provides a good chance of missing it altogether or perhaps receiving a glancing blow. If the vehicle in front of you starts to slide, it is usually better to brake first, remembering the risks involved when braking heavily while cornering, to wipe off some of your own speed, then prepare to steer around the other vehicle. The other vehicle will be taken by centrifugal force towards the outside of the bend, so aim to get by on the inside if for any reason you cannot pull up first. Never try to brake hard and steer simultaneously.

10

JUNCTIONS

Once you recognise that accidents do not 'just happen' of their own accord but are caused by bad driving, you will see that there is no reason why they cannot be avoided. Roads meet and diverge in all sorts of ways, such as crossroads, T-junctions, roundabouts, forks, and it is here that the motorist faces extra risks. But by applying the techniques of advanced driving and using a systematic approach, it is possible to negotiate them as uneventfully as any other part of the road system. Extra care is called for, but it is also wise to bear in mind that junctions present other road users with an ideal chance to 'do it all wrong' and many of them would appear to be waiting for this chance to try their own peculiar ways of approaching and navigating such a hazard. We must be on our guard, then, for what a road safety expert has aptly described as 'an accident looking for somewhere to happen'.

It is at crossroads that there are most opportunities for error, either on your part or on another road user's. If you are approaching on the minor road, or if neither road has precedence, you must plan ahead and be prepared to stop even though the signs may tell you only to give way. If there is room for two lines of traffic on your side of the road, it is essential to start moving into the correct one at an early stage, checking the mirror and signalling accordingly. Stay in the left-hand lane if you intend to go straight across, since keeping in the right-hand lane can dangerously mislead other motorists. Even if there is insufficient room for doubling up the traffic lines, it is still better to edge over to the side corresponding with the route you will follow as you leave the junction.

If you are going straight ahead or turning left then it is merely a matter of waiting until the road is clear to right and left, checking that nothing is approaching from the opposite minor road, and then moving off smartly. But a word of warning: an oncoming vehicle may be signalling to turn, which could lead you to think he will bear

The sign says 'Give Way' but, as is clear from this picture, it is often better, even necessary, to come to a halt. A surprisingly high number of accidents occur at points like this, whereas sensible driving would avoid trouble. Advanced motorists think about these situations in advance.

off at the crossroads and therefore not interfere with your intended path. Take care, though, because direction indicators do get left on by mistake and the driver may be planning to go straight ahead, without realising that he is telling other road users otherwise. If you pull out in front of him and there is a collision, the law may favour him rather than you, so it is not safe to assume that a vehicle will turn until you actually see the driver begin the manoeuvre into another road.

When turning left, you may find yourself becoming impatient as you wait for a gap in the traffic. A chance might arise – a gap you can slip into if you accelerate hard and the driver behind slows down, but don't do it. This sort of driving is discourteous at best and can be nothing short of dangerous. It can so easily lead to an accident if your engine hesitates or the other driver is slow to react. Again, it will be your fault, and all for the sake of shaving a few seconds off your journey time. You know the saying: it is better to be a few minutes late in this world than a few years early in the next.

Right turns at crossroads are governed by the same basic rules about not pushing in, and not taking turn signals for granted. If opposing traffic is also turning right, there can be a moment's confusion as drivers decide whether to pass nearside-to-nearside or vice versa. You will notice that the favoured method seems to vary not just around the country but even from one junction to the next along a busy road. However, there can be only one safe rule, unless the road layout or white lines dictate otherwise: pass offside-to-offside. This may limit the number of vehicles able to get through a right turn in one traffic light sequence, and it calls for the car at the end of the line to hang back, but it does mean that each driver has a clear view down the road ahead as he makes the turn. In the nearside-to-nearside approach, each driver has to nose blindly out across the traffic stream, hoping, since he cannot see for certain, that no one is approaching or, if they are, that they will stop. It's easy to see why so many accidents happen when a driver is turning right.

Travelling on the major of two routes at a crossroads does not mean you have the right to drive as you like. It is necessary to apply the rule of courtesy and consideration towards other road users, but beware of putting politeness before practicality. Many drivers are willing to stop to let someone out of a side turning. That's fine, but if they are in a line of fast moving traffic it can cause a lot of disruption and possibly even an accident. This is because the people behind you will not be expecting a sudden stop, and will be taken by surprise. So misplaced courtesy can be dangerous. It is best to stick to the rules and accepted practice of the road even if it means that someone has to wait a little longer to get out of a side road.

When traffic lights control the junction it is asking for trouble to drive on as the red light comes on, or even to anticipate the change to green by moving away on amber. At some traffic lights, the all-red phase is quite long and you might be lucky, but at others it isn't and you could meet another driver trying just the same dodge from the opposite direction. And do not forget that inconsiderate driving like this can catch pedestrians unawares. Local authorities do not usually give much advance warning of filter lights ahead, and you may find yourself sitting at a green left-turn filter when you want to go straight on. Even a brief pause will inevitably bring angry horn blowing from behind. It is possible to sit there waiting for the all-green phase, but it is more courteous to turn left and find an alternative way of getting back onto your route.

Right: The correct (*above*) and incorrect (*below*) procedure for turning right on a two-way road when faced with an oncoming car with the same intention, whenever possible. The lower diagram clearly illustrates how severely the 'nearside to nearside' method restricts your vision.

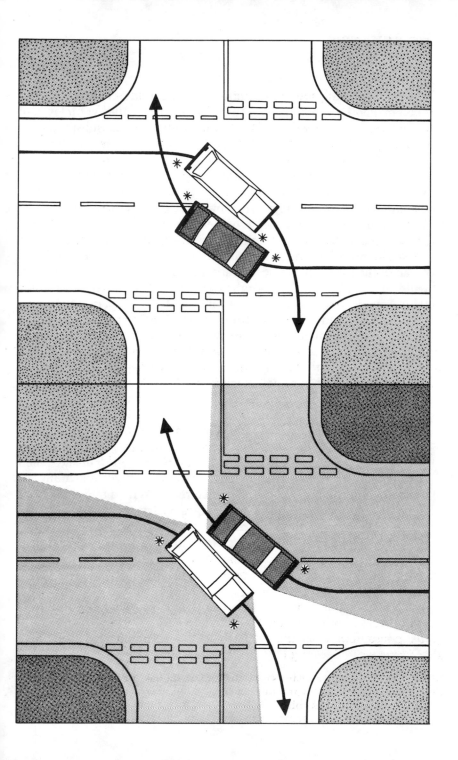

Equally, this applies at T-junctions. You should not allow yourself to be misled by unintentional turn signals from other vehicles, and do not shoulder your way out into the traffic on the assumption that other drivers will see you and slow down to let you in. Many T-junctions have a mini slip-road, which in theory at least can be used to build up speed so that you can merge easily with main road traffic. Most of these acceleration lanes appear to be made on the assumption that modern cars are very narrow and have tremendous acceleration. Their main use is in obviating the need for a near-90 degree turn out into the main road. Treat them with care – stay back if you have any doubts – and if it seems wise, stop and wait until there is a suitable break in the traffic. Some acceleration lanes *do* work well, if they are wide enough and long enough to accommodate something more than a motorcycle. Yet many motorists treat them as a double-white-line halt spot and stop accordingly. Occasionally you see this even on motorway approach roads. In such a case, try to build up speed quickly and move out into the main road early – as long as it is safe to do so – to be in the main stream when you pass the timid driver.

Hanging back at roundabouts can be just as unnecessary. Large ones usually carry fast moving traffic but give you plenty of time to slip into the nearside lane and build up your speed as you join the flow. Small roundabouts may provide less of this acceleration space, but most vehicles negotiate them so slowly that you need less room anyway. Spare a thought for road engineers, who design their roundabouts for maximum flow and easy entry, only to see motorists queueing unthinkingly at the approach roads. With a few exceptions – such as places where walls and hedges obstruct vision – it should be possible, traffic allowing, to enter most roundabouts with only a slight reduction in speed and a change to a lower gear, checking as you run up to the entry point that there is nothing coming from the right. Traffic already on the roundabout has right of way, with a few exceptions.

When a major route passes through a roundabout, the local

Right: How to tackle a roundabout. Notice that if you intend to take the first exit (*top*) or the second (*centre*) then the inside lane is for you, because you will not then have to change lanes whilst going round. However, the outside lane (*bottom*) is the right one for you if you are to take the third exit. Always signal your intentions clearly, but not too soon, as you can easily confuse those behind you. However, with signalling, common sense must prevail.

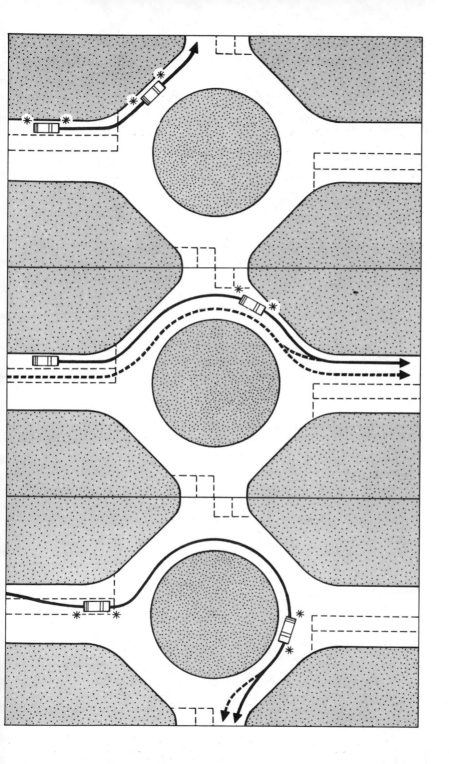

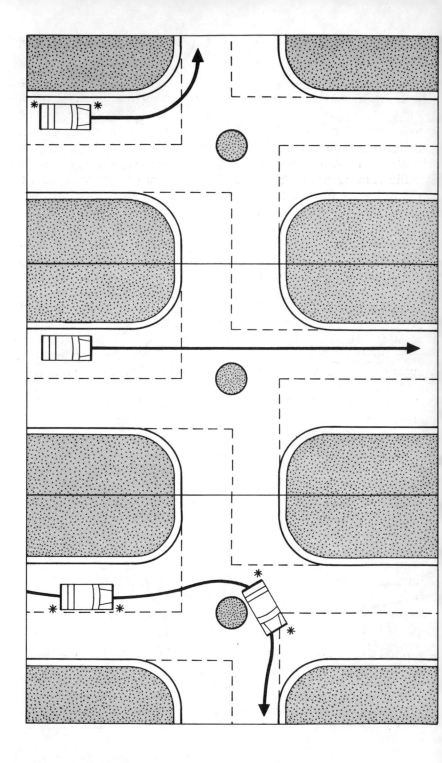

authority sometimes gives it priority by putting up signs and painting a few white lines on the road. For those who know the road, it works well and helps to speed the traffic flow. But for the stranger to the area it can come as a shock to discover that, believing he has priority on the roundabout, he is suddenly expected to stop and give way to traffic coming from the left. Traffic lights are sometimes there to add to his confusion. The way to reduce the risk is to stay in your correct lane and remember your signalling procedures, so that everyone on the road around you is aware of your intentions.

An increasing number of junctions have been turned into mini-roundabouts, and these often prove very successful in reducing traffic queues, since they give vehicles on the busiest roads a fairer crack of the whip. As on full sized roundabouts the majority – but not all – entail giving way to traffic approaching from your right: priority to the right in fact. But many motorists still seem unclear about this rule and equally shaky about their real or supposed rights once they are actually on the roundabout. As more than one local authority road safety officer has observed, the chief benefits of mini-roundabouts may lie in the fact that almost all drivers are unsure of the correct procedure on them, so everyone slows down and takes extra care.

Established practice and lane lines mean that you keep to a more circular route on large roundabouts. Unless the roundabout is an unusual one or has special markings, you should keep to the left if you are taking the first exit, signalling a left turn all the way through. When your exit is more or less straight across, try to keep over to the left as you enter, keep over to the nearside and start signalling a left turn at the exit before the one you are taking. If the traffic has forced you over to the right on entry, stay there but take care not to cut in front of anyone when exiting. For later exits, enter on the right, stay there and move over to the left as you approach your exit. Signal a right turn before entering the roundabout and continue to do so until passing the exit before the one you want, at which point start signalling left.

Left: How to negotiate a mini-roundabout. The procedure for taking the first exit (*top*) is much the same as an ordinary left turn, though extra care must be taken to watch for traffic coming from the right. For the second exit (*centre*), no change of course should be necessary, though caution should again be exercised in regard to traffic from both right and left. The third exit is taken in exactly the same way as a full-size roundabout.

11

SIGNALS

Signals are not the same as orders, as many motorists seem to believe. They must never be used in such a way that the driver will then assume that everyone else is going to give way. Police officers will tell you that the comment they hear most frequently at the scene of an accident is 'But I gave a signal' from the motorist who has caused the trouble. Visible and audible signals are the motorist's only way of communicating with other road users, apart from CB radio, which does not apply to learning the art of proper signalling. It is fundamental to good driving that we give the right signals at the right time and in the right way. But no one should lose sight of the fact that signals can only inform: they cannot instruct.

We agree that this is a complex part of good driving, and to become totally familiar with it demands practice as well as learning. As with so many things, the basic rule is a simple one: use only those signals given in the *Highway Code*. Do not make up your own, or copy other drivers; although such signals may seem perfectly clear to you, they could be dangerously misleading to someone who sees them for the first time and is expected by you to react to them. Even if your signal is correct in every respect, never expect everyone around you to see it, interpret it correctly and act on it sensibly. It's always best to assume that other motorists may not have done so, and to drive accordingly, than to take their recognition of your intentions on trust.

Signals employing the direction indicators are the ones most commonly used, and can of course be adopted for manoeuvres other than turning left or right, to help other road users realise what you are doing. For example, if you intend to turn right at a set of traffic lights, signal your intention early so that motorists behind have plenty of time to pull into the inside lane and pass you on the nearside as you slow down. Keep the direction indicator winking if

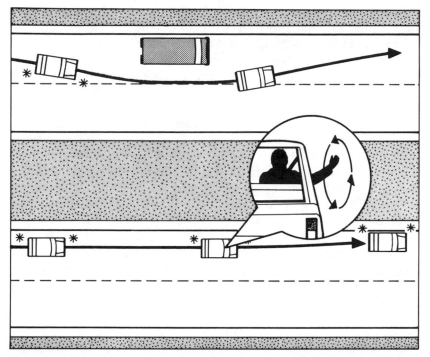

Overtaking (*above*) and stopping on the carriageway (*below*). Notice that when overtaking it is seldom necessary to signal left when moving back in front of the overtaken vehicle. When overtaking, you should be travelling in a straight line.

   When stopping on the carriageway, a signal is enough where it is obvious that there is no left turn ahead. This will avoid confusing others, but the *correct* hand signal doesn't do any harm.

your right-turning traffic stream comes to a halt. This will prevent drivers behind you who want to go straight on from getting in the wrong lane.

   When overtaking, keep the right turn signal on until you start to move back to the nearside, as its flashing will help oncoming drivers to spot you from a distance. It is quite unnecessary to signal a left turn as you move back to the left-hand side – as many motorists do – unless an unforeseen development ahead forces you to cut in abruptly (and this should not happen with good planning).

   At one time, it was deemed normal and polite to tell other drivers you were moving in and stopping by a circular wave of the hand.

This practice is rare nowadays and has been replaced by a simple left turn signal on the direction indicator, which is acceptable and adequate in nine out of ten cases. But in the tenth instance, the driver behind may be so close or the traffic situation such that he might benefit from a more emphatic warning of your intentions. That is the time to wind down the window and give an old fashioned hand signal.

Occasionally, you see drivers who mean well but give an incorrect slowing down signal. Instead of the 'I am pulling into the kerb' rotary wave they give the 'I am stopping – *you should too*' up-and-down movement with the hand facing downwards. They would probably be quite surprised if you did pull in behind them, as the signal indicates, and walk up to ask why they had stopped you. The right time for the signal is when, after watching him in the mirror, you think the driver following you is either too close or driving inattentively, and therefore might not realise you are coming to a halt in traffic. The signal is particularly appropriate when you stop at a pedestrian crossing.

In the same way, left and right turn hand signals are only needed these days to emphasise your plans to other road users whom you believe might otherwise miss them. For example, you might do this when two turn-offs are close to each other and you want to make it clear which one you are going to take, or to show that you intend to turn right and are not just pulling out to pass a stationary vehicle. The arm signals for left and right turns are still used sometimes and to signify 'I am going straight on' for the benefit of traffic controlling police. So although hand signals are rarely used, when they *are* required the need is urgent.

However well disposed you may feel to other road users, there are two signals which you should never use. One is the 'You can overtake me' wave to a following vehicle, and the 'Please cross' to pedestrians on a crossing. Both are omitted from the *Highway Code*, simply because from your position in the driving seat it is impossible for you to judge whether it is safe for other road users, whether at the wheel or on foot, to do anything. Leave it to them to make the judgement – to encourage them to rely on yours is at best risky and might even make you liable at law for any injuries they may receive in an ensuing accident. Irresponsible drivers are increasingly eager to break the law and overtake on either side of traffic halted at a crossing, so this applies more than ever.

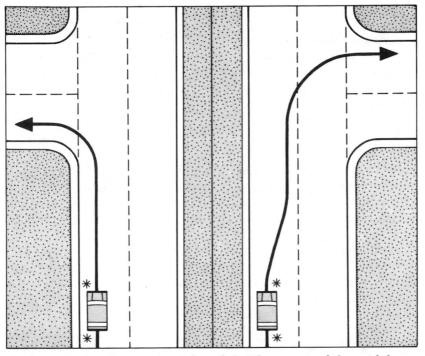

The lines to take when turning right or left. When turning left, avoid the unnecessary action of veering off to the right before negotiating the bend. Massive vehicles may *have* to do this (watch it if you are driving behind one) but it is pointless and dangerous when driving a car. For the right turn, move over to the crown of the road in plenty of time, and be patient if the oncoming traffic is heavy.

Headlight signals should also be avoided, as they do no more than say in effect 'Don't forget I'm around'. Even then, use them with great caution because of the considerable risk of a misunderstanding. Many motorists take a flash of the headlights to mean 'Look out – I'm coming through', but many more use and therefore interpret it as 'Although I'm on the main road, I'll slow down and let you come out of that side turning'. You can see the problem when a member of the first school of thought meets a follower of the second. To add to the confusion, truck drivers have their own complex system of headlight flashing. A flash of the lights from one lorry to another that is in the process of overtaking the first means 'The tail of your vehicle has cleared the front of mine. You can pull back in to the nearside now.'

Therefore, with a great many people reading a number of different meanings into the simple act of flashing the headlights, it is hardly surprising that confusion arises. The Department of the Environment's official ruling is that headlights should be used as a signal only to draw the attention of other road users to your presence. That's fine, but until every motorist understands it, drivers should be especially careful not to leave their intentions open to misinterpretation.

Much less misunderstood are brake lights – their message is abundantly clear and, of course, automatic. But other opportunities arise when you can use them to convey additional information to other drivers. A driver whom you consider to be following you too closely may drop back to a safe distance if you brake lightly at first, which gives him plenty of time to react before you have to brake at all firmly. Such a warning can pay off if you are the last car in a line of traffic stopped unexpectedly, as on a motorway or just over the brow of a hill. By applying the brakes regularly, even when the car is stationary, the lights will flash a warning to the next driver that the vehicles ahead are not just moving slowly but are at a standstill. Don't forget that brake lights are just as likely to fail in one or both bulbs as are direction indicators. It is easy to check both sets of lights by trying the signals at night with the car backed up close to a wall or to another vehicle. If the lights are working correctly you should see the reflection clearly enough by craning your head round.

Much simpler to check is the horn, as this needs only a quick toot (but don't forget that it's illegal to sound it between 11.30 p.m. and 7.00 a.m. in a built-up area or at any time of the day or night if the car is stationary). In an emergency, such as to avoid an accident, it is not illegal. As with the headlights, the horn is there only to inform other road users that you are around. You might give a polite tap on the button to warn children playing in a residential street or an absent-minded driver starting to pull out of a side turning in front of you. However, it should never be used as a substitute for the observation, planning and courtesy that are the hallmarks of a good driver.

It is often a good idea on a main road to give a slightly longer note when overtaking, especially when passing a lorry in which the cab is so noisy and vision to the rear so restricted that the driver probably hasn't noticed you. This practice of sounding the horn as you come up to overtake is widely used in some Continental countries, but much less so in Britain. It must therefore be used with discretion, as many drivers react remarkably badly to the sound of another vehicle's horn. Some treat it as an insult, a reprimand, or a challenge – according to how and when it is delivered – and react accordingly. Sensible use of the horn is what counts. It may not be used often but it is there for a purpose and to believe that it should never be operated is a mistake.

12

DRIVING AT NIGHT

Some motorists who have just passed their test put off driving in the dark for as long as possible, but night driving is an essential part of motoring for the majority of people. Like any other aspect of handling a car safely, driving when it is dark presents no undue risks if you observe the rules. In fact, there are positive advantages to night driving for, as the traffic thins out, your journey time is reduced and that can mean a worthwhile saving when you are making a long journey. Naturally, driving in the dark can be dangerous if you don't stick to the rules, especially on a long – or perhaps overnight – run. There are a number of measures that need to be taken because accident rates rise dramatically at night.

Your car, of course, should be in good order, with headlights working on both dipped and main beams. If you are in any doubt, get them adjusted by a garage. Adjustment at home is possible but can be difficult, and therefore the general rule is that this is a job best left to the professionals. With a full load of people and luggage, the car will be weighted down at the back, and the nose will be pointing up a few degrees. This is enough to put the main headlights completely out of adjustment, with the dipped beam where the main ought to be and the main pointing up to dazzle oncoming motorists and illuminating the tops of hedgerows. Some cars have a simple device for clicking the headlights down to a position which overcomes this, but most vehicles don't. So if you are planning a long trip at night, you should get your garage to adjust the lights, but don't forget to have them reset when you return.

Ask someone to walk around the car to check the side, tail, brake and turn signal lights for you, or you may be able to see the reflected light if you park close to a wall. On the road you can check the lights again from time to time when stationary in a line of traffic by looking for the reflection in the chrome of the cars ahead and behind.

There are some worthwhile changes that can be made if you are not satisfied with the standard lighting system for your car. On most modern cars you can switch over from the conventional tungsten lamps to quartz halogen ones, which give a much more powerful and much 'whiter' light. Auxiliary lights, of the fog or spot type, are worth having but they must be carefully aimed, especially if you set the spot to illuminate the nearside kerb and the foglamp to light the centre of the road. These must be used together – a single beam of light is illegal since it could be mistaken for a motorcycle's – and they have to be mounted within the dimensions laid down by the Department of the Environment. By law very low-slung lamps can be used only in conditions of fog or falling snow.

Be seen at night. Many drivers are content with using their sidelights in a built-up area after dark (*left*) but as the picture (*right*) so clearly shows, dipped beams are preferable. They not only increase your own vision ahead, for some street lighting is less than ideal, but – more importantly – they allow you to be seen better by other road users.

If you have a movable spotlight for reading signposts, make sure it does not have a rigid handle sticking down into the car. In an accident, you might hit your head on it. And don't forget it is illegal to move the spotlight about when the car is running.

Reversing lights are essential at the back. If your car does not have them fitted as standard, you can buy them at accessory shops and wire them into the system to come on automatically when reverse is selected.

Extra-bright ancillary rear warning lights are a definite boon in conditions of poor visibility, if only to avoid the classic rear-end collision in which the offending party claims that he didn't see your lights in time to stop. Equally worthwhile are supplementary brake lights, which can be bought as an accessory for mounting in the rear window. Their main advantage lies in the fact that, due to their high location, a driver several cars back in a stream of traffic is given a much earlier warning when you brake.

Most cars these days have a switch which will set all four direction indicators flashing simultaneously when you have to stop at an awkward spot in an emergency. They can also be bought from accessory shops.

Yellow bulbs or glass should never be fitted to the headlights. They are compulsory in France, where they are found to cut down dazzle, but that is only because they reduce the amount of light coming from the bulb. It's not that yellow is in some way less dazzling than plain 'white' bulbs, but simply that the partially opaque colouring reduces the total light output. Other European governments do not favour yellow headlights, and neither should you.

It is just as important to make sure that the driver, as well as the car, is properly prepared for night driving. There is a warning in Chapter 8 of the dangers of 'night driving' glasses. They, or ordinary tinted sunglasses, should never be used after dark. Just like the yellow headlamps, they might reduce glare but they also cut down the total light. Wearing them means that you might fail to notice an unlit cyclist in the shadows. Myopia (short-sightedness) and other sight deficiencies get relatively worse after dark, so never take any chances here either. Remember it is an offence to drive with defective and uncorrected eyesight. Should you be in any doubt, an optician will be able to test your eyes for night driving purposes and may prescribe spectacles accordingly.

Few people – professional truck drivers apart – regularly drive long distances at night. It's important to prepare yourself properly, otherwise what could be an enjoyable journey along near-deserted roads and through sleeping towns can turn into a nightmarish struggle to stay awake at the wheel.

Start by not working too hard during the preceding day, and take only a light meal in the evening – a heavy one will make you drowsy before you start. Never take pills to stay awake, since such drugs can have dangerous side-effects on your driving. Needless to say, don't drink any alcohol.

Always break the journey with regular stops every hour or two.

That's quite long enough for you, and more than enough for most passengers before they want to get out of the car to exercise cramped limbs by walking around for a while. You may feel yourself becoming very tired in the later stages of the journey, so stop the car (being sure to get right off the road) and try simply dozing off. A few minutes' sleep can be a wonderful reviver. Better still, go for a short but really vigorous run up the road and back to get your circulation going again. All being well, you will not reach a state where you have to resort to these extreme measures. Fatigue at the wheel can be as lethal as driving under the influence of drink or drugs. But don't forget that it is illegal to stop on the hard shoulder of a motorway. By keeping the heater on and building up a pleasant fug in the car, you make the job of staying alert all the more difficult. It is best to keep fresh cool air passing through the passenger compartment, even if it

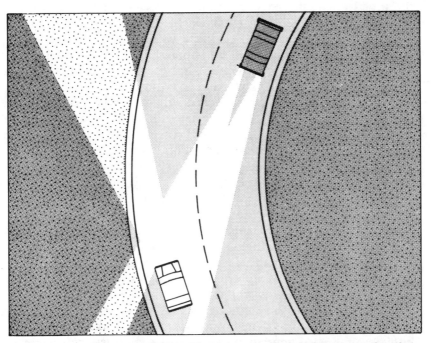

Courteous use of the main beam. The driver on the left doesn't need to dip his lights in this situation, because his beam will not strike the oncoming car. The driver on the right should dip his lights to avoid dazzling the first driver.

means having diagonally opposite windows open to keep a strong current going.

One of the most common complaints about night driving from novice drivers is the glare from approaching headlights, which we have already discussed in Chapter 8. As your experience of night driving increases you will find that your eyes are drawn involuntarily towards the headlights of oncoming vehicles. A conscious effort is required to look away and concentrate your gaze on the road straight ahead, but in time you will find that approaching headlights actually help you to see more of the road ahead for yourself. From time to time you will meet a motorist who is too thoughtless or ill-mannered to dip his lights. One should, of course, dip early and certainly before the other vehicle is within range. If the other driver does not respond to your dipping action, it is permissible to remind him with a quick flash back to main beam, then down to dip again. But however strong the urge to retaliate, never stay on main beam: this makes for two dazzled drivers on the road instead of one, which in turn means twice the danger. Remember also that, while the human eye quickly contracts the pupil to shut out unwanted light, it takes much longer to dilate again afterwards. For several risky seconds you will be driving in a semi-dazzled state, and so will the other motorist.

It is essential to keep your speed down, even when your eyes are functioning properly, so that you never drive beyond the range of vision. You are heading for trouble if you cannot pull up within the distance illuminated by your headlights. Keep your headlights on main beam on country roads, unless you are approaching other road users – and that includes cyclists and motorcyclists, just as much as car or truck drivers. If you pass a vehicle coming the other way on a left-hand bend remember to dip early to avoid your main beam sweeping across the curve and dazzling the other driver. Conversely, your headlights are shining out towards the outer edge of the curve on right-hand bends and so should not come anywhere near an approaching vehicle. Many drivers are unaware of this and will be waiting for you to dip your lights as you approach. Be courteous, and consider doing so even though it may not actually be necessary.

Keep your headlights on dipped beam when following another vehicle, otherwise your main beam will dazzle the driver via his mirror. And switch to dipped beam when following two-wheelers, as their riders find their own visibility is impaired if their shadow is thrown forward by a main beam.

You should keep the vehicle ahead at such a distance that it is in the far fringe of light from your dipped beam, remembering that a safe stopping distance must also be maintained. Keep your speed down when on dipped beam, as the reduced visibility must inevitably mean a reduction in stopping distances as well.

Raise your hand to the mirror if the driver behind is selfish enough to keep his lights on main beam. Don't keep it there, though. If he doesn't respond after a second or two, dip the mirror. If your car is not fitted with a dipping mirror, move the mirror a degree or two out of adjustment so that his lights can still be seen in it but do not blind you. With either mirror, remember to readjust it afterwards.

Use dipped headlights, rather than sidelamps only, in anything but the most crowded and brilliantly lit towns. They should also be kept on for illuminated urban motorways and in bad weather. Never hesitate to turn on your sidelights as soon as daylight begins to fade, and use the headlamps as soon as you consider them necessary. Surprisingly, a lot of drivers seem to obtain some satisfaction from keeping all lights off until the last possible moment and you will be given a reproving 'flash' if yours have been switched on. These people obviously do not realise that at dusk and after nightfall those lights are there as much to ensure you are seen as for you to see by. Put your lights on early: they cost nothing to run and will not shorten the life of your battery. Be sure to keep the glass clean to make the most of the illumination, for even a thin film of mud can cut light output by half, while only a tenth of the light may get through a thick film.

13

TYRES

Most people are aware these days of just how important tyres are. Gone are the days when they were regarded merely as being round, black objects with a hole in the middle. Nothing else seemed to matter; but nowadays motorists and manufacturers alike have a different attitude towards tyres. The industry has spent a lot of money on developing tyres which will enable motorists to drive more safely, and which will last longer. Today's tyres have characteristics, especially in wet conditions, which would have left previous generations gasping with disbelief.

It is sensible to understand something about tyres, since those four footprints of tread we mentioned earlier are your only contact with the road. You will have to buy a set sometime anyway, unless you change your car regularly. There are two main categories of tyres:

Cross-ply tyres used to have the market to themselves and are still available, although mainly in lower price brackets. Their name comes from the fact that the fabric beneath the tread patterns is arranged with diagonal plies, each alternate ply being arranged on the alternate diagonal.

Radial-ply tyres have become much more popular in the last 20 years or so and now dominate the business. More expensive than cross-plies, they last longer – in fact, they usually work out cheaper in the long run because they outlast the cross-ply by such a large margin. The radial gets its name from the casing which has its plies arranged in a radial pattern. It is braced by a steel or textile band running around the outer circumference. There is little point here in going into the finer technicalities but the net result is a tyre which gives much better roadholding and handling than the cross-ply. While radial tyres no longer mean a harder ride, they still look underinflated when pumped to the right pressure.

Many motorists fail to understand the mass of 'secret' markings

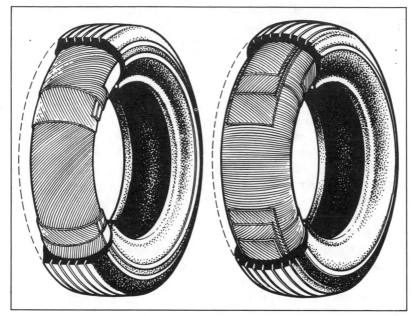

The difference between a cross-ply (*left*) and radial tyre (*right*).

which cover tyres, and it is hardly surprising. First there is the size, which may be 165/70×14. All that means is a tyre of 165 section, a 'low profile' (70 per cent of the normal, in fact) to fit a 14-inch wheel. For the man actually buying the tyres, the units of measurement used by the manufacturers for the size (not to mention the mythical 100 of which that profile is 70 per cent) is a source of mystery. To complicate matters still further, other figures indicate the maximum speed at which the tyre can be driven safely. These are indicated by a code of letters indicating speeds of 130mph and more, which with today's traffic and speed limits is little short of academic. It has never been satisfactorily explained by a tyre manufacturer why the speed ratings cannot be indicated in simple figures. Nor has a clear reason been advanced as to why comparable cross-plies come with a slightly different set of maximum speeds, not to mention a totally separate system of marking.

Not surprisingly, most motorists buy a set of tyres which are duplicates of the ones supplied with their cars. Should you be tempted to be more adventurous, here are some points to consider.

It is normally well worth trading up from cross-plies to radials. Few modern cars will not take them but, to be absolutely sure, check the owner's handbook, look at the tyre maker's fitting list or ask the car manufacturer.

Never mix tyres. If you have two radial and two cross-ply, the radials must be on the rear wheels. Any other arrangement is illegal and dangerous.

You *can* still save money by purchasing remoulds, but make sure they come from a reputable company. These are made by taking a worn but sound tyre and moulding a new tread on it – hence the name. Remoulds are best suited to cars which will not exceed 70mph. They should never be fitted to high performance models, nor on ordinary cars if you are going to the Continent, where speed limits are higher. Similarly, second-quality tyres are sometimes available but are hardly to be recommended.

Do pay the extra charge to have the wheels balanced when the tyres are being fitted. The fronts will benefit further from the costlier dynamic as well as static balancing. An out-of-balance wheel can make the steering or the whole car vibrate unpleasantly, even at 50mph.

To get the best out of new tyres it is necessary to run them in, and a maximum of 50mph for the first 100 miles is usually enough.

The economy of buying inferior tyres could prove a false one. Don't do it. On the other hand, do not allow yourself to be browbeaten into buying better tyres than your car and style of motoring require. You wouldn't fit remoulds on a Ferrari: don't put expensive VR tyres on a small family saloon.

Sports-style wheels are popular nowadays, but bear in mind that alloy wheels are much more prone to damage and corrosion than steel ones. Those which are wider than the wheels they replace can throw a considerable extra strain on the hub bearings, which then need to be replaced correspondingly quickly. Wider wheels and tyres will sometimes improve roadholding, at least on dry roads, but the disadvantages are heavier steering and a harsher ride. If too wide, the tyre can rub on bodywork when the car is driven around a corner or over a bump, and that can be dangerous. Should you make this change, buy from leading tyre companies (they also produce the wheels in many cases) and take any advice offered by the car manufacturer.

It is all too easy to damage any kind of tyre you fit by careless

This photograph shows the distortion that a tyre is subjected to when the car is cornered at full lock at 25mph. This sort of treatment will wear your tyres out very quickly. PHOTO COURTESY OF DUNLOP LIMITED

driving. Locking the wheels when braking, scorching getaways and quick cornering will all wear the treads more rapidly. And driving over kerbs, or scraping them, can cause serious internal damage that will not show on the outside, yet could cause sudden tyre failure at that crucial moment.

Since tyres are expensive it makes sense to look after them properly, so drive with care and keep them at the right pressure. It is important to follow the manufacturer's instructions on this and not to experiment, as you are not likely to improve on his findings and might well come a cropper instead. Pressure checks should be carried out at the beginning of a journey when the tyres are cold. On the road they warm up under constant flexing, which heats the air inside and sends up the pressure. The makers allow for this, of course, and it would be wrong to test the pressure at this point and 'bleed' it back to normal by letting some air out.

It is well worth buying a good quality pocket gauge in an accessory shop and using only that for your measurements, since garage pressure gauges do tend to vary. Before a long motorway run, or if you are carrying a full load of passengers and luggage, remember to increase the pressures by the recommended amount (if any).

Don't alter pressures to cope with unusual conditions. Lower pressure will give you less, not more, grip in mud and snow and you

Four examples of abnormal tyre wear caused through neglect. Periodic examination of your tyres can spot trouble early enough to prevent it becoming a problem.

Left to right: The result of underinflation – insufficient pressure in the tyre has put all the load on the shoulders, resulting in excessive wear.

This tread has worn away completely, and incorrect wheel adjustment has produced feathering of the tread edges.

Another example of incorrect wheel adjustment, this time leading to wear running sideways across the tread.

What happens when you overinflate. The tyre takes an over-round shape, producing rapid wear in the tread centre. PHOTOS COURTESY OF DUNLOP LIMITED

will also spoil the roadholding, and may even damage the tyre when you get back on the road. It is possible to make a slight improvement in fuel economy by raising pressures above the correct level but this will reduce roadholding, especially on wet roads, and – as with an underinflated tyre – can lead to uneven tread wear.

All being well, tread wear will be even across the width of the tyre. If it isn't, first ensure that the tyre hasn't been inflated wrongly, probably due to a faulty gauge. Failing that, either the steering or the suspension is out of alignment, which ought to be dealt with by a garage.

By law, worn tyres must be replaced at the latest when the tread grooves over threequarters of the tread width are down to their last millimetre. Anyone with an eye for safety will recognise that this level is remarkably low, and will think about a replacement when the rubber is down to the 3mm mark. Simple gauges are available to

The Denovo Safety Wheel, developed by Dunlop. The components (*top*)
are bolted together to form the wheel, and if the tyre punctures, the inside
of the flat tyre touches the buttons on the containers, which release a
lubricant to prevent friction and also to help to seal the hole. They also
release some vapour which reflates the tyre sufficiently to allow it to be
driven on for up to 100 miles at speeds up to 50mph. The picture *below*
shows the wheel fitted to a Rover. The tyre has sustained a puncture, but is
still at sufficient pressure for safety. PHOTOS COURTESY OF DUNLOP
LIMITED

measure this accurately. A worn tyre is unable to move water off the road quickly enough and this is the main reason for changing early. If the rubber is to bite down onto the road at 60mph a tyre has to get rid of gallons of water every second. Much of the water is moved by being picked up in the grooves and slots of the tread and then flung out behind as the wheel rotates. Once the tyre is worn, its ability to squeeze the water away is diminished. A bald tyre can shift very little water and quickly rides up onto the surface – a condition known as aquaplaning, because the tyre is shooting along on a film of water and not touching the road at all. The result is a total lack of steering control if the front wheel is involved, in addition to zero braking. Even a sound tyre can aquaplane momentarily if driven fast over a deep puddle. If you have done this, you will have felt the steering go momentarily light in your hands.

Worn tyres not only give you less grip in wet conditions, but are also more prone to punctures. Deflation is rare these days, though even a good tyre may puncture. If this happens, change to the spare (the pressure of which, hopefully, you have remembered to include when checking the other four) and continue. A garage can perform a temporary repair on punctured tyres with a rubber plug but this is a measure only to get you home, pending a proper job by a specialist. You should never drive a plugged tyre far or at excessive speed, and *never* drive for any distance with a flat tyre, as that will ruin it.

There should be no problem about bringing your car to a halt after a puncture even if you are travelling fast, providing you brake gently and try to steer more or less straight ahead, just moving to the left as you stop. Some steering is maintained, even with a front wheel puncture, as long as the deflated tyre is not rolled off the rim by a violent movement of the steering wheel. Most accidents involving the tyres are caused by harsh braking or swerving after a puncture, fitting tyres of the wrong type, overloading them, or running them in an already damaged condition. The cause of many motorway tyre failures is insufficient pressure. The tyre flexes too much, each movement builds up more heat and finally rubber begins to melt and the tread comes off the casing.

14

OVERTAKING

Each part of the overtaking manoeuvre is related to one of the basic aspects of safe driving and therefore several are covered elsewhere in this book. However, there are some points to bear in mind which relate specifically to overtaking.

First, there is the basic question: ask yourself whether the overtaking manoeuvre you plan is strictly necessary. It will be justified, if safely performed, if it is to pass a slow-moving vehicle which is genuinely impeding your progress. However, if the sole purpose is to move up one place in a line of traffic, then what point can there be? Consider, then, whether the operation you plan is motivated by the practical consideration of improving the progress of your journey or whether it is simply an instinctive desire to get ahead.

After 'why' comes the all-important 'when'. It is likely that overtaking will mean you have to spend some time on the wrong side of the road, so careful planning and rapid thinking are essential, together with decisiveness. Ask yourself whether the road is clear far enough ahead for you to pull out, overtake, and pull in again without inconveniencing the vehicle you are planning to pass. Overtaking can be a lengthy business, even if you are using full acceleration. If an approaching vehicle comes into sight from around the bend or over the hill that forms the horizon of your vision, you could be in trouble. Remember that, if you are travelling at 60mph and the overtaken vehicle is doing 40mph, you will be overhauling it at only 20mph. If the vehicle bearing down on it from the opposite direction is travelling at 60mph, the rate at which he is closing on you is 120mph (60+60). You do not need to be a skilled mathematician to realise that, unless your timing is right, a very dangerous situation can quickly develop.

Of course, this should not be taken as a reason for not overtaking at all but there are certainly grounds for planning the operation with some care and not with an air of optimism. In addition to allowing for traffic on your route, you must also be prepared for the motorist who might come out of a side-turning, drive or lay-by, pause at the main road, look to his right to check that nothing is coming in his own lane, and then pull out. It is a fact that far too many people fail to look *both* ways, as they never think that an overtaking vehicle may be approaching them from the left in the right-hand lane. It is, of course, impossible always to allow for such a situation in advance but it is an important point to watch while overtaking. If a vehicle *does* appear from a side road, give him a quick toot on the horn and/or a flash of the headlights to draw his attention to you.

But to return to the basic overtaking manoeuvre itself, the next point after checking the 'why' and 'when' is the 'how'. Once you have satisfied yourself that there is ample room ahead, you should check the mirror before starting to pull out. At this point we assume you will not be so close to the vehicle ahead that you have to move out just to look at the road ahead. If there is no one behind who is about to overtake you, and no one coming up on the outside – and possibly out of range of your main rearview mirror – give a right turn signal, change down if necessary to a gear that will give you maximum acceleration, put your foot down firmly but smoothly and start to pass. Ideally the gear you select will be one that enables you to complete the entire operation and return to your own side of the road before the engine revs are so high that it is necessary to change up. This will ensure that you are able to keep both hands on the wheel throughout the exercise.

As you draw level with the rear of the vehicle you are overtaking, keep a wary eye open for any signs of intended deviation from course. Watch the driver, who may be thinking about overtaking the vehicle in front of *him*, or turning right, and is more than likely to start either manoeuvre without even glancing in his mirror or considering a signal. If he starts such a manoeuvre, or if you have even an indication that he might, give him a short sharp blast of the horn. In fact, it is considered quite normal in some Continental countries to 'toot' as you overtake in order to ensure the other driver is aware of your existence, and it is a pity the same practice is not customary in Britain.

Some people resent being overtaken. They may shift down a gear and accelerate as hard as possible to keep you behind them. Even more dangerous, they may close the gap ahead of them to shut you out in the right-hand lane. This is, of course, insane behaviour, but never fall into the trap of trying to retaliate, either by outracing the other driver or carving him up by forcing your car ahead of his. Remember that two lost tempers are twice as dangerous as one. You must treat such appalling behaviour in the same way as you would react to it outside the car. Just pull back into place behind him. Happily, such behaviour is infrequent. Almost always, the other driver will let you through, and then it is up to you not to cut in sharply in front of him. Do keep a watchful eye on your mirror. As soon as the overtaken vehicle starts to appear in it, there is more than enough room for you to complete the manoeuvre and return to your own side of the road.

15

DRIVING IN WINTER

It is important that every driver knows how to cope in winter conditions. Although British winters can be mild, sooner or later you will have to face treacherous roads when driving. It is essential to make sure that your car is in good shape and able to meet the demands imposed on it. Learn how to drive properly in snow and ice, as many people forced to abandon their cars in bad weather could carry on if they knew what to do.

Tyre grip is the first priority in winter. You will find that a pair of knobbly treaded 'town and country' or 'mud and snow' tyres on the driving wheels can help a good deal, but you must have a safe mix of ply types. And remember that these tyres help only in the softest going such as mud or fresh snow. In other conditions, the limited amount of tread rubber they actually put on the road surface can be a disadvantage. The majority of motorists would do better to keep their ordinary tyres and carry a set of chains or straps which can be slipped on when conditions become extreme. Modern grip improvers can be fitted quickly, unlike the old-fashioned chains, but do practise fitting them at home before you have to do it in a blizzard. To work effectively, chains and straps need a layer of snow between them and the road surface. When you find yourself on clear road again, they begin to wear out quickly and do nothing for your road grip so take them off without delay. It's also possible for a worn chain to gouge chunks out of your wing.

A small shovel kept in the boot is often useful for gathering roadside grit to spread under the driving wheels if you – or anyone else – runs out of grip on a hill. A useful idea is to carry a couple of sacks, and a length of string with which to tie them to the door handles. You put them under the wheels for grip then, once the car is rolling again, you can press on until level road is reached before stopping to pull them into the car. But it is important to ensure there

These Norwegian 'Snowgrips' are one of the aids available to motorists in a sticky situation. Easily fitted and removed, they provide the necessary grip that a car needs in poor conditions, and are an improvement on the old chains, which can easily snap if worn and damage the car's bodywork.
PHOTO COURTESY OF NEWSPRESS

is enough string to allow the sacks to trail clear of the back wheels once the car is rolling.

Adhesion is important, of course, but so is visibility. Another piece of sacking should be carried to put over the windscreen if you have to park for more than a few hours in freezing temperatures. To combat ice on the side windows, use either a plastic scraper or de-icing fluid, both of which are widely available. Most new cars are fitted with a heated rear window, but if your car does not have one, buy an element as an accessory. Fill the windscreen washer bottle with a proprietary fluid that cleans and de-ices, and do keep the head, side and tail lights as clean as the windows.

Study the manufacturer's handbook and learn how to make the

One method of getting traction on snow or ice is to tie sacks to the door handles of your car, and then drive over the sacks, having ensured that the rope is long enough to let the sacks trail free of the car once you have got going. This way you will not have to stop to retrieve the sacks until you have reached firmer ground.

most of your car's heating and ventilation system. Modern systems enable you to warm the car while keeping the glass free from condensation, even with a full load of passengers. It may occasionally be necessary to open the windows a little – perhaps half an inch – to keep a good supply of fresh air circulating. It is still possible to see drivers wiping a smeary gap to peer through on a misted windscreen: this is inexcusable and quite unnecessary. Equally dangerous, however, is allowing the interior to get so warm and stuffy that there is a danger of the driver drifting off to sleep.

In Chapter 12 you will find the basic aspects of night driving, but for winter use auxiliary illumination is desirable or, in some cases, essential. On this issue the law is complex and changes from time to time. The best legal compromise is a pair of fog lights, preferably

A special tyre for special conditions. The Avon 'Winter Sport' incorporates lateral biting edges for extra grip on ice and hard-packed snow and wide slots to expel slush and water. PHOTO COURTESY OF AVON RUBBER COMPANY

with quartz halogen bulbs, mounted at the regulation height of between two feet and three feet six inches (anything lower can be used only in thick fog or falling snow).

A mixture of one spot and one fog lamp, using the former's more concentrated beam to light up the nearside kerb, is favoured by some drivers. Others like to have secondary lights wired into the headlamp circuit to give coupled illumination. The final choice is always a personal one, perhaps influenced by trying the cars of friends already equipped with one or other of the systems described. Whichever type you favour, there is no doubt about the requirement at the back. You need a large reversing light which is switched on and off automatically by the operation of the gear lever, and a large bright additional rear lamp or two to give warning to those behind you in fog. In a modern car, there should be a hazard switch that will set all four flashers blinking to warn other road users if you are forced to pull up in a dangerous spot. Most garages can supply and fit such a switch if your car doesn't have one.

Several other details about driving in winter should also be noted, including topping up the radiator with a water/anti-freeze mixture. Plain water will dilute the anti-freeze already in the system.

A lock which has frozen overnight can be thawed by a key heated with a match.

Salt on the road thaws the snow and ice but it can ruin the metalwork of your car. Try to hose the underside clean when the milder weather arrives.

Keep an eye on the temperature gauge if you fit a radiator blind or metal foil over the grille to aid rapid warming up on winter mornings. Modern cooling systems and thermostats in good working order are not affected by our winters. In fact, it's easy to overdo things and restrict the flow of air to such an extent that you can create overheating problems.

Now for the driving. Everything should be done smoothly and gently – a good idea in normal conditions but absolutely vital when the surface is slippery. A skid is generally started by jerking the steering wheel suddenly or by stamping violently on the brake pedal. Skids can usually be avoided by more careful operation, so start each steering movement extremely gently, especially on snow or ice, and use the same method with the accelerator and brake pedals. Skids involve either the front or rear wheel tyres losing their grip, although all four wheels might end up sliding. Rear wheel skids are the more common, and are usually the result of cornering too fast or piling on too much power, so that the wheels start to spin. They produce an unnerving sensation as the car starts to move sideways as well as in the direction you had expected. But it's only unnerving if you don't know what to do.

There are many theories about the way to cope with a skid, but there is just one correct system and it's the one practised by experts such as traffic police and top racing drivers. First, don't panic and stand on the brakes: that will only make matters much worse. It will not slow you down but it *will* put the car even further out of control. So stay well away from the brake pedal. The correct procedure is to lift off the accelerator to remove the slide-provoking power from the wheels, and steer into the skid. So if you are on a right-hand bend and the tail is therefore swinging out to the left, you have to steer to the left. This opposite lock, as it is called, will pull the car back into line, but don't hold it a moment longer than necessary or the tail will slide out the other way. As the car corrects its course, start paying off the steering ready to resume steering to the right again. If you are too

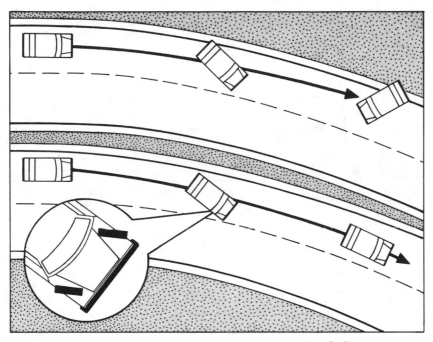

The rear wheel skid and its cure. In the *top* example, the skid is
uncorrected, and the inevitable spin occurs. The competent driver will
steer in the same direction as the rear swing (*bottom*) and thus cancel it.
The manoeuvre calls for neat judgement with the steering wheel, or an
even worse opposite skid can result.

slow, a series of pendulum-like slides, first one way and then the
other, will build up as you over-correct the steering. But even that
may be better than doing nothing at all, in that it will eventually
slow your progress somewhat. If left totally unchecked, the car
will skid off the road completely or, just as serious, collide with
something.

Front wheel skids are less common, but not so easy to remedy.
They occur when the front tyres lose their grip while the ones at the
rear retain theirs, and this causes the car to plough on in a straight
line when it ought to be turning or stopping. One possible cause is
over-heavy braking that has locked the front wheels and robbed you
of steering control. The answer is simple — release the pedal then
reapply it with less pressure, or with the on-off technique described
in Chapter 6.

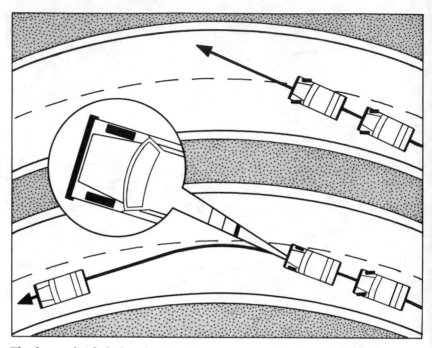

The front wheel skid and its cure. Uncorrected, this skid will take you away from the curve you wish to follow, with potentially disastrous results. The solution to the problem is to steer into the skid, feet away from the pedals, to enable the front tyres to resume their traction. Once this has happened, further attempts can be made to steer your desired course, though fine judgement is needed at the wheel. Over-correction can lead to a pendulum-swinging effect on the rear of the car, which can be just as dangerous as the original skid. Most front-wheel skids are caused by lack of judgement on the part of the driver, though sometimes one can be forced on you by circumstances, so it's vital that you know how to cope.

It is also possible that the skid is caused not by braking but by turning the steering wheel too sharply. This breaks the tyres' grip on the road, and the solution is more difficult. You must steer towards the straight ahead position so that the wheels can start rolling again, then start steering once again in the required direction. It may sound simple, but the catch is whether there is enough room and time in which to do it.

Ideally, get some experience of controlling a skidding car by going along to a skid pan. In this way, your first taste of the sensation comes in safety with an expert instructor at your side. Motorists who have accumulated this kind of experience in safety are much more able to react properly if they get into a skid on the public road. Ask your local authority road safety officer if there is a skid pan in your area.

The important subject of tyre grip in winter does not end there. Braking technique is described in Chapter 6 and the precautions taken when driving on wet roads must be applied even more rigorously when you are driving on ice or snow. You must allow a much greater braking distance between you and the vehicle in front. On ice the space needed to pull up can be 10 times that required on a dry road. It's too easy to be lulled into a false sense of security when the section of road you reach is free of ice or snow. Around that next bend the road might be as slippery as before, and you may find yourself with 50 feet in which to pull up when you need 500. . . . Speed is relatively easy to add on, but hard to take off.

Of course, all this assumes you have managed to get the car moving. If you can't, it may well be because of tyre grip problems, caused this time by trying to push the car along rather than slow it down. Even the best tyres can easily lose their grip and start spinning when the surface is slippery, and this can happen just as easily in the mud of summer as the snow of winter. This happens partly because the treads become filled with ice (so you can see that badly worn tyres are even more risky at such times) and partly because water, whether liquid or frozen, is unfortunately an ideal lubricant between road and rubber.

The answer is to supply the wheels with just enough power to start the car moving but not so much that they start spinning. The higher the gear the less the grip-breaking power, so always try to start in second instead of first (using second or mid-range ratio on an automatic). The accelerator must feed in just enough power to prevent the engine from stalling. And you must do everything with as much finesse as you can manage. Should the grip be lost and the wheels start to spin, you must at all costs fight back the temptation to depress the accelerator still further. This only makes matters worse, and helps the wheels spin themselves down into the quagmire until the back of the car is eventually resting on the ground and there is no hope of salvation, short of a tow or digging it out.

You may gain a foot or two before the wheelspin starts. If this happens, let the car roll back, dig away any loose snow or obstructions and try again. This time you should progress a few more feet. Given patience and skill, enough of a runway can be won, going back to the end every time, for speed to build up high enough for you to drive out of trouble and on your way again. Your passengers can help by spreading grit, brushwood, sacks or even the car mats under the driving wheels to improve traction. If this works, don't stop to pick up people or tools until you are in the clear.

It is important to keep in a higher gear, not only when getting out of a tight spot, but also when driving on ice or snow as it helps to ensure that you will not feed too much power into the wheels and precipitate a skid. Try to use one ratio higher than normal, with proportionately less throttle opening, but do be careful not to let the engine labour unduly.

Now we have looked at the techniques for coping with roads when they are in a bad condition, there is one other aspect of winter motoring to be considered. That is the importance of reading the road in order to anticipate really bad spots before they catch you out. Even on a fine day, ice can form where trees shade the road or the wind sweeps across an exposed hilltop.

Learn to recognise the notorious but often misinterpreted black ice. This is water that has melted during the day, spread across the road and then frozen at nightfall into a smooth coating with all the grip of an ice rink. At first glance in the headlights you may not even notice that the road is different: it may simply look wet. Black ice can be very frightening and should be treated with the utmost respect.

As we have said before, learn to develop your powers of observation. In this way you will stay clear of the many troubles that can be encountered when driving in winter. But, of course, even the most prudent motorist can find himself hopelessly stuck on a country road. Should this happen, you have a straightforward choice: wait for help or go and look for it. Your decision will depend on the road. If you can reasonably expect another vehicle to come along in the next hour or so, then wait. But don't make the potentially fatal mistake of leaving the engine running and the heater switched on for too long. Many exhausts leak small amounts of gas which are normally blown away unnoticed by the slip-stream of the car when travelling. But when the vehicle is stationary for a long time the gas seeps into the passenger compartment, where already tired occupants are beginning to doze in the warmth. There are large quantities of poisonous carbon monoxide in exhaust gas and, as it is devoid of all taste and smell, it is easy to see how it can be lethal. Perhaps a better solution is to get out of the car, after making sure as best you can that it is not obstructing other road users, and start walking. As you make for the nearest building which looks likely to be inhabited, wave down anyone you see on the way.

16

DRIVING IN SUMMER

Each season brings pitfalls for the driver, and there are almost as many hazards awaiting you during the sunny days of summer as there are in winter. In summer, a film of dust, oil and rubber will quickly build up on most road surfaces in dry weather. On its own this does not present too much of a problem, but add a summer shower and the result is a greasy coating that can be almost as slippery as ice. When the first rain comes after a long dry spell, take special care. After a while the rain washes away the coating and the road does in fact become less, rather than more, slippery, even though the amount of water has increased. However, it's still wise to take it easy.

While it doesn't usually last too long, summer rain can be very heavy. If your windscreen wipers are having problems coping with the deluge in a thunderstorm, it may well be foolhardy to continue your journey. And be prepared for roads which become flooded because of a blocked drain. When this happens, it is much more sensible to stop and wait for the worst of the storm to pass. After all, you can only continue at a greatly reduced pace and, with visibility and tyre adhesion already below acceptable limits, there is a high risk of running off the road or being in a collision with someone less careful than yourself.

Do take precautions against the high humidity that accompanies summer storms. These mist up your windscreen and you will probably have to switch on the defroster to clear it. Perhaps you will also have to open two diagonally opposite side windows to start a through-draught. While this may let in the rain, this is preferable to driving half-blinded by steamed-up glass.

If you decide to continue your journey in a storm, there is a danger that you will encounter flooding, although this happens more frequently in the winter. Floods and fords can be negotiated quite easily as long as you observe some basic rules. First, check that the depth is not so great as to flood the engine. A foot of water will do no harm to most cars and some will cope with twice that depth if handled properly, although the owner is likely to have water seeping in through the doors. Anything deeper, especially if it is above the base of the engine cooling fan, should not be attempted. The fan blades will pick up the water and spray it over the ignition, producing a short circuit which will leave you stranded.

Use banks, hedgerows and even buildings along the side of the road to assess the depth of the water. If you are convinced it is shallow enough to be negotiated, start in first gear and keep the revs high to prevent water running down the exhaust and stifling the engine. If necessary, slip the clutch to keep up the revs. Make sure you enter the water slowly so that you don't build up a bow wave that could splash back over the engine.

Even if you take these precautions, there is still a chance that you will get stranded as a result of water on the ignition system. If this happens, you may do best to get out of the car through an open window, rather than by opening a door and letting the water in. Wade round to the boot for the spark plug spanner, and then to the engine to remove the plugs. Once they are out, it should be possible to drive the car out on the starter motor. Engage bottom gear and keep the starter turned on until you reach dry land. This method involves ill-treatment of the engine, and the starter motor will need to cool down every 15 seconds or so, but it will get you out of trouble. Unfortunately, it is a trick that does not work with automatic transmission.

The next problem will come once you leave the flood water behind. Water seeps into the brakes and renders them virtually useless. While discs are not too badly affected – the moisture on these can be cleared away with a few hard jabs on the brake pedal – the drum type found in many cars for the rear wheels are more troublesome as the water can stay there for some time. Solve the problem by driving slowly, and braking hard regularly, while being careful not to impede any traffic which may be around. It is possible to drive along in first gear while keeping light pressure on the brake pedal with your left foot. Be careful if you do this, because your left foot is much less sensitive than the right and it is easy to apply the brakes too harshly.

These problems aside, summer and holiday motoring can be made more agreeable if you travel overnight and avoid the worst of the crowds. If you do this, ensure you have sufficient rest before starting and on the journey itself, otherwise you can get dangerously tired.

Keep your windscreen clear of the film of dead insects and traffic dirt which builds up by adding a washer additive liquid to the water in the reservoir. A ball of newspaper is also remarkably effective for wiping away traffic film.

17

DRIVING FOR ECONOMY

With the price of petrol increasing so dramatically in recent years, all motorists are now giving more thought to economical driving. Most motorists are aware of the arguments in favour of energy conservation, quite apart from their desire to save money by visiting the filling station as infrequently as possible. However, this quest for economy, although it is to be encouraged, must never be allowed to take priority over considerations of safety. It is easy to allow this to happen and to find yourself in a potentially dangerous position because you allowed petrol saving to become more important than planned, systematic and constructive advanced driving.

There are a number of do's and don'ts to follow when trying to make the most of each precious gallon of fuel.

● Don't inflate the tyres to a higher level than that recommended by the manufacturer. While it might save you a few drops of petrol, it wears out the tyres more quickly and – more to the point – it reduces the grip and therefore the roadholding, braking and steering.

● Don't use fuel of a lower grade than the right one for your car. This can lead to serious engine damage.

● Don't stay too long in the higher gears, especially when the road speed demands a lower gear. To do so defeats the advanced driver's precept of always being in the right gear at the right time.

● Don't coast in neutral, either down hills or when coming to a halt. It means you are in no gear at all and could not hope to accelerate out of trouble if the need suddenly arose.

● Don't drive unnecessarily slowly. You will be a hazard to other road users and to yourself.

● Do keep speed down to what could be termed the minimum reasonable level.

● Do ensure that, as far as the need to be in the right gear at all times allows, you don't rev the engine too fast.

● Do make sure the choke is closed as soon as possible after a cold start (assuming your car does not have an automatic choke) but at the same time keep the engine running properly. Closing it too early can cause loss of power and possibly a stall, which is potentially dangerous if it happens at a spot such as a junction.

Always try to buy a car with a fifth gear, or overdrive, especially if you do a lot of main road driving. The additional high gear can help to save money on fuel bills, and will eventually pay for itself if it's an optional extra.

Check whether the car you plan to buy comes in a choice of engine sizes. The smaller unit is likely to be more economical, though in some instances it has to work so much harder that in practice it consumes as much petrol as a bigger but underworked engine.

Compare fuel consumption figures of the cars you have put on a short-list before purchase. Many of these statistics appear in the weekly motoring magazines and in the Institute of Advanced Motorists' own *Milestones* magazine. Don't be misled by the manufacturers' figures, even though they are the result of Government approved tests. The steady 56mph figure, for instance, can look very good but is unlikely to be attained in real life. Fuel consumption figures are reduced mainly by starting up and accelerating, but you can hardly avoid accelerating if you are to drive safely. Quite apart from getting away from rest and overtaking, constant speed fluctuation is an inescapable part of motoring.

You can, however, try to time your journeys to avoid heavy traffic, since crawling along in a queue is very bad for fuel economy. Keep the engine in a good state of tune – out-of-adjustment ignition and carburettors are wasteful. Ask your garage to check, too, that the brakes are freeing off properly and not rubbing, and that the wheels are correctly aligned.

The grade of petrol you buy could save you money, as well. The correct one for your car is the cheapest grade that does not cause 'pinking' – the destructive pre-ignition during acceleration that is apparent from a faint tinkling noise. Using a higher grade than your car needs is pointless, as it does not produce more power for your engine. Its extra cost goes entirely on the chemical additives that resist the pinking.

Diesel cars use much less fuel than their petrol-engined counterparts, in exchange for a drop in performance and increase in noise levels (admittedly, not great with the latest designs). They are popular on the Continent, where diesel fuel is often very cheap. In Britain, however, diesel fuel is not cheap, and diesel cars cost much more to buy, so you have to cover an enormous annual mileage before showing a net saving.

Few accessory economy devices consistently give any measurable improvement. After all, if they did, the car manufacturers (who are especially interested in good mileage figures) would adopt them. Most of these devices will only restrict the amount of petrol going into the engine, which will be partially starved and start to lose power if the amount falls below the correct one. Therefore, in saving money, you lose performance and have to open the throttle further to regain the required speed – and consequently you'll need more fuel again. However, there are one or two possibilities you may consider. Some carburettor and ignition kits increase engine efficiency and could be expected to repay their cost in time. And there are engine tuning companies which will work on your engine to gain a similar increase in efficiency. Bear in mind that it will take a long time to recoup the cost in terms of petrol saved. Most accessory shops sell an 'engine efficiency meter' (or vacuum gauge) which can be worth fitting. This measures the depression in the inlet manifold and translates this into a simple item of information which is shown on the facia dial. You will find that by balancing the accelerator opening against road and engine speed you can keep the needle in the part of the dial that shows you are making the best use of the fuel for as long as possible while remaining consistent with considerations of safety.

The best economy device costs nothing at all: it's your right foot. You save a lot of petrol by avoiding excessive acceleration and feathering the accelerator back when you have reached cruising speed. A car will cruise comfortably in most conditions on surprisingly small throttle openings. There will be only a marginal increase in speed by putting your foot further down, and much heavier fuel consumption.

18

TRAFFIC

Ask yourself when planning a route whether travelling on crowded roads is a strictly necessary part of your journey. In nine out of ten cases the answer will probably be 'yes', but occasionally you might find that, by re-timing your journey or planning to by-pass towns (this can be achieved by travelling on country roads as much as on purpose-built by-passes), you can avoid the traffic altogether.

If your route leaves you no alternative but to drive through congested areas, do try to make life as easy as possible for yourself. You can, for example, reduce the amount of concentration needed for navigation. A passenger will probably be happy to guide you across a strange town by map reading, and street plans are often printed in the margins of better road maps. If you are driving alone, make things easier by planning the route in advance and writing it on a card at which you can glance when you are stationary at traffic lights. A route card, perhaps written on the back of a postcard, might read like this:

At Westerham turn l. onto A25
5 miles later turn l. onto A21
Then immediately r. onto A25
4 miles later at Seal turn r. towards Godden Green
Then immediately l. towards Stone Street

It is possible, with the aid of a suitably scaled map, to judge the distances fairly accurately and then correlate to the mileage figures coming up on the car's speedometer to warn yourself in plenty of time when you ought to start looking out for the next junction.

Every motorist will find that a certain amount of driving in traffic is a part of life and, since it cannot be avoided for long, it is best to learn to live with it. Familiarity with heavy traffic conditions can lead to a dangerous over-confidence, which you must guard against at all costs.

It is main road traffic which usually seems the most daunting, with two or three lanes of traffic travelling along at anything up to 70mph. Few of the drivers are likely to keep a proper distance behind the vehicle in front, and you will inevitably see the type of driver who shows he is in a hurry by switching lanes. Always keep a safe braking distance, even if it means that people drop into the space you have left and force you to drop back further. This measure will make very little difference to your journey time, but it could ensure that you do not collide with another vehicle if anything untoward happens further along the road.

Lane-swopping is discouraged in most countries, but in Britain it seems to have become an accepted but none the less unwelcome and risky aspect of driving. The inside lane is normally for slow vehicles, those who stop frequently (usually buses), and anyone proposing to turn left. The centre lane is used by traffic proceeding straight ahead and at a reasonable rate, while the right-hand lane is for overtaking and making right turns. Trouble comes when people see that traffic appears to be moving faster in the lighter-loaded right-hand lane and pull into it, only to be forced to wait when they come up behind someone turning right. It is advisable to treat two-lane roads as though the outside and centre lanes of a three-lane road were combined. So stay in the inside lane unless you have a specific reason for temporarily occupying the right-hand one.

Keep an eye open for left-turn filters that allow the inside lane vehicles to leave early at approach junctions, especially those controlled by lights. If you find yourself in a left-hand filter lane when you want to go straight on, it is best to make the turn and then get back on your route via side roads. To sit tight with drivers behind you blasting their horns is not dangerous but is certainly discourteous.

In traffic, keep checking your mirror, even when stationary at traffic lights. A vehicle coming up behind may not have realised that you have stopped, and a few quick dabs on the brake pedal will alert him to your presence when he sees your brake lights flash.

On a hill, the vehicle in front might roll back. There's not a lot you can do, apart from sounding your horn and easing off your own brake a fraction so that you absorb some of the impact – but take care not to roll back yourself. Learners – and some more experienced drivers – have been known to engage reverse instead of first, so leave them plenty of room.

It should be unnecessary to state that rushing across traffic lights as the signal changes to red is lethally dangerous. Just as risky is starting to cross when the lights change to amber, if only because another motorist might have decided to nip across the junction as *his* lights change to red. Remember also that the green should not be regarded as an authority to proceed, only as permission to continue with caution.

When you have stopped, put the handbrake on and shift the gear into neutral. As soon as you see the amber to green sequence, engage first gear and prepare to release the brake. Many motorists waste their own time and that of other road users – not to mention reducing the traffic capacity of junctions – by delaying these operations until the green has actually appeared. While you are waiting, watch the lights rather than gazing around you so that, when they change to green, you will be ready to move on and will not have someone behind you blasting his horn.

Don't hold the car on the clutch if the stop is on an uphill stretch – use the handbrake. The former method wears out the clutch rapidly, while there is a danger that you will stall the engine and let the car run back.

There is quite likely to be oil on the road at traffic lights and other places where vehicles stop, so make allowance for a possibly greatly reduced grip of the tyres, both in terms of braking and of accelerating away again. And remember that a thick coating of oil and rubber deposited on city streets and polished by the constant passage of tyres makes them likely to be more slippery in wet weather.

Watch out, too, when the pavements are crowded because even experienced drivers, away from their vehicles, are quite likely to step out into the road without even a glance to see whether it is clear. And beware the cyclist who comes out of a side street without even looking. Never forget the High Court ruling that a cyclist is entitled to wobble about in the road. It is the motorist's responsibility to avoid him.

Keep to the left in one-way streets unless that lane is heading towards a left turn or you have plans to bear right yourself. It is permissible to overtake on the left in a one-way street but this might take other road users and pedestrians by surprise. You can also overtake on the left in slow-moving traffic if you are in the inside lane and the right-hand one is travelling less quickly. But 'inside overtaking' on main roads which happen to have one carriageway separated from the other (as on a motorway) is not allowed unless your line of traffic is moving more rapidly than the right-hand lane. On motorways it is also strictly forbidden to use the hard shoulder for overtaking.

Do take special care when you come up behind traffic waiting to turn right. While there may be room for you to slip through, do so with extreme caution. There might be a pedestrian stepping out between stationary cars and not thinking that any vehicle might be moving in his immediate vicinity. And a driver in the right-hand lane might suddenly pull over into the lane you have joined and go straight on.

At a pedestrian crossing it is, of course, a serious offence to overtake the leading vehicle.

Two important rules relate to parking: observe the law, no matter how unreasonable it might be (bear in mind that many parking restrictions are actually intended to discourage you from using the car in town) and, secondly, consider the safety and convenience of other drivers and pedestrians. Such consideration might take the form of not parking in front of someone's drive, or not leaving the car where people using a popular crossing spot will have to funnel around it.

Once learned, the technique of parking is really remarkably simple yet somehow it evades many throughout their motoring lives. The way to get into a space is to drive alongside it, and assess whether it is long enough to accommodate your car. Then move half a car's length forward until the *middle* of your own vehicle is approximately level with the *back* of the one ahead, keeping about two feet out. Start to reverse slowly on full left lock (if on the left-hand side of the road). As the front of your car clears the one ahead, switch to full right lock and carry on reversing. Performed correctly, this will take you into some surprisingly small gaps. It is then only necessary to centralise your car by edging forward a few feet with the wheel centred.

This parking technique works well anywhere but there are some aspects of urban and traffic driving that vary from one part of the country to another. London motorists have a style which seems almost foolhardy but it works well because they tend to be decisive. They know what they are doing: they *think* they know what others around them are doing. The press-on approach helps move massive volumes of traffic through some outdated road systems. The same

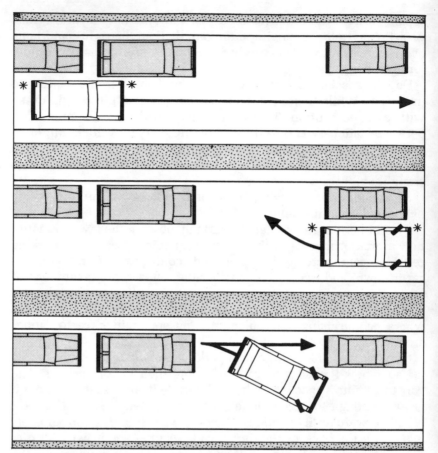

Parking in a restricted space. This is one manoeuvre which many drivers never master, yet it is simple, and is a good way of demonstrating a driver's spatial concepts. Provided that you have judged the available space accurately, this procedure should be completed in two movements – first backwards then forwards – though a bit of juggling might be called for in a really tight situation.

method applied in provincial cities looks boorish if not actually dangerous, simply because the driving style is out of place. In the same way, some provincial drivers are shocked by the goings-on at somewhere like London's Hyde Park Corner in the rush hour. So the advice can really only be: 'When in Rome, do as the Romans.' Even if you think the driving style is odd, there can be all sorts of problems if you fail to conform to the existing traffic pattern.

19

MOTORWAYS

Motorways are now a well established and totally integrated part of our road system, but somehow the media and even a few drivers continue to hold them in an awed respect that borders on the morbid. Everyone knows that bad accidents can happen on motorways, mainly because of the attention focused on them by television and newspapers. The point is that a motorway accident reported in the media is likely to be catastrophic, and it is sometimes forgotten that motorways have a much better accident record than any other main road. The chances of an accident on a motorway are much lower than one on a comparable non-motorway trunk route. The motorway, therefore, should get you to your destination not only more quickly, but also more safely. But you have to stick to the rules, and possibly help to avoid some of the disasters that other motorway drivers sometimes seem determined to cause.

Our own views on motorway driving are based on experience and, of course, the rules and guidelines laid down in official publications. They are further influenced by the comments and advice we have obtained from the most professional of all professional drivers: the police patrol officers.

You have at least two things going for you on the motorway: there are no intersections and it's strictly one-way, so you will not have someone nipping across your bows or coming the other way. Or will you? There are instances on record of drivers, apparently otherwise sane, who have passed their exit and U-turned across the central reservation to recover their position. There have also been cases of people who have managed to drive down an exit road the wrong way and set off along the outside lane in the wrong direction. Thankfully, such examples are rare, but you can't be sure you will never see such a thing yourself. What action should you take if you are unlucky enough to encounter a driver like this? We can only recommend taking avoiding action first, then headlight-flashing and arm-waving to warn the madman and finally stopping at the next emergency phone (they are a mile apart) to tell the police.

Bad driving is more likely to be the worst hazard you will find on the motorway. Here is some advice to ensure that your own driving comes up to scratch even if others fail to meet the standard.

In the slip road approaching the motorway, accelerate to build up speed to that of the traffic on the inside lane. Signal a right turn, so that anyone in that lane will notice you, then slip into place. On the way in, keep an eye open for anyone at the end of the slip road who is waiting for a large gap in the traffic flow. These people are as big a menace to other road users as they are to themselves.

You should stay in the inside lane for at least half a mile or so, checking the mirror to establish the traffic pattern behind you. If it is a three-lane highway and you are in a car as opposed to a commercial vehicle, your cruising speed will probably be better suited to the central lane. After the usual signal and mirror check, move over into the middle lane. If the inner lane is reasonably clear, remain in it until you wish to overtake, returning to it when the overtaking manoeuvre is completed. The third lane is not the fast lane that many people imagine it to be, and is there only for overtaking.

Your speed should be one at which you, your passengers and the car feel comfortable, and which is appropriate to the weather and traffic conditions – but it must not be over 70mph, of course. It does not matter if it's well below the limit. You will find a few miles per hour clipped from your speed will make little difference to a journey time, and 70mph should be treated as a limit, not a target.

Should a motorist coming from behind be travelling at more than 70, we should not try to stop them exceeding the limit. Baulking an overtaker, legal or otherwise, is bad manners and can be dangerous and the police would not thank you for it, anyway.

When you have settled into a steady cruising speed, keep glancing in the mirror and maintain strict lane discipline. The constant lane-changing seen on urban motorways, and occasionally on rural ones, saves the driver little time, yet makes it much more likely that he will cause an accident. Drivers do not expect to be overtaken on the inside and this is dangerous, as well as being a serious offence.

Keeping a safe distance between you and the vehicle in front is even more important than good lane discipline. Elsewhere in this book we have explained why it is essential to leave room for seeing, reacting, and braking, and this is especially relevant on a motorway. We know it is all too easy to close up on the vehicle ahead until the distance between you is nothing like enough in an emergency. One reason why people fail to keep a safe gap is that the sensation of speed becomes dulled and, in addition, overtaking vehicles tend to slot into the space you have allowed. All you can do is drop back accordingly.

Almost every autumn there is a multiple pile-up on a fogbound motorway, usually as a result of people driving too fast for the conditions. But there is rather more to it than that. A driver may have been keeping a safe distance behind the next vehicle, based on the assumption that the leader of the string of vehicles will himself have a fair distance in which to stop, and will warn by his brake lights when he does. But this assumption can be lethal. The leader may be stopped instantaneously and without warning to those following by piling into a crash. In fog, you must allow for the stopping distance which you need under these conditions.

In other respects, driving in fog on the motorway is governed by just the same rules which apply to fog driving on other roads: keep your speed down to whatever gives safe braking distance within your range of vision, keep well to the left (do not follow central lane markings), put headlamps on dipped beam for day or night (remember you need to be seen as well as to see), open windows, turn on the demister and wipers to keep the screen free of moisture. Above all, retain a philosophical approach. It is better to turn off at the next exit and wait for the fog to clear, even if that means a night away from home, than to end up a victim in one of those terrible nose-to-tail crashes.

The use of dipped headlights in daylight should not be restricted to foggy conditions. The law now states that we should do the same as Continental motorists, notably the Germans, and switch on dipped beams whenever it rains or visibility is otherwise diminished. The object of this exercise is to ensure that you are seen more than to improve your own vision. Headlight beams attract attention to the rear-view mirror, so drivers further up the road will have earlier warning that you may soon want to pass them.

The growing network of automatic signals on motorways does not cater for heavy rain, although they will warn you of fog and accidents ahead, providing you can translate the curious codes used. We hope our diagrams will help but we fail to understand why motorways

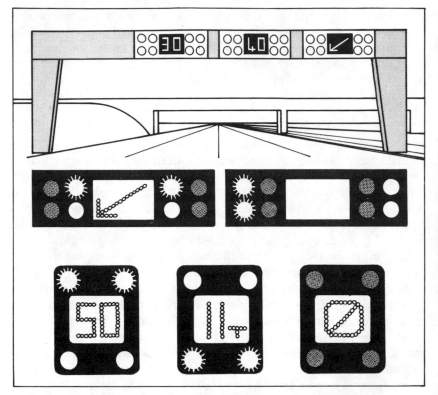

Some motorway signs. The *top* part of this diagram illustrates the gantry which displays the signs, which in this case are showing speed restrictions and an imminent lane closure on a three-lane carriageway. The *central* part of the drawing shows how the various restrictions are accompanied by flashing lights. The *lower* part shows other signs that you may come across on the motorway, displaying, *left to right*: temporary speed limit, outside lane closed ahead, and the 'clearway' sign, which is not accompanied by flashing lights, to show that the temporary restrictions have finished.

can't have simply FOG, CRASH or CLEAR indications. There is no reason why the light patterns could not be switched on to allow this, and it would certainly make life a lot easier for motorists. As it is, even the STOP sign is far from clear: the flashing red lights used to show this are something we associate with a warning to cut speed rather than a direct order to halt. But they must be obeyed, in the same way as the temporary speed limits (to be treated as limits and not targets). Of course, not all people understand these limits, let alone respect them. When you see a car approaching from behind it pays to assume that it is travelling fast and to delay any planned manoeuvre of your own until it is out of the way. As it's almost impossible to judge the speed of a vehicle approaching from behind, extreme caution should always be exercised.

Exiting from the motorway is achieved through a simple procedure. With the early warning signs giving way to closer ones, and then the three-, two- and one-bar signs leading you into the slip road, it is obvious you must synchronise your speed with that of the nearside lane. Slot into place (but not before checking your mirror and signalling a left turn) ready to exit at the right moment. But beware as you enter the slip road, as this is a potentially hazardous moment. Many are designed for speeds well under 70mph, and after driving for an hour or perhaps half a day at around the legal limit, your judgement will be seriously impaired. Fifty miles per hour will seem more like 30mph, and it's all too easy to approach the roundabout and start to brake on the basis that you are travelling at the lower speed. Do take care with your speed when leaving the motorway, otherwise hazards will possibly take you by surprise.

Equally, it is possible to become 'speed happy' while still on the motorway and perhaps to attempt a violent swerve in an emergency which you would never normally try at such a high speed because of the risk of starting a skid.

Motorways often cut through exposed countryside and for this reason there is a danger of becoming caught in powerful cross winds. As soon as you feel one tugging at your car, reduce your speed to a level at which it is easy to steer a straight course without constantly veering across the road at each gust. Too firm a grip on the wheel will cause the car to wander, so retain a light hold. It's also possible to adapt quite unconsciously to the side wind by applying a little corrective steering lock. It may be that a degree or two of right lock will be needed to keep the car moving in a straight line against a wind blowing from the right. But when you pass into the shelter of a bridge or cutting, or when you overtake a large lorry, the corrective steering will no longer be necessary. It is quite likely that the car will move across the road for a yard or so if you have not prepared for this by unwinding the steering as the wind pressure drops. You will steer automatically to correct this, as you come out into the wind again, since the car will yaw the other way unless you have again anticipated the effect and steered to balance the car against it.

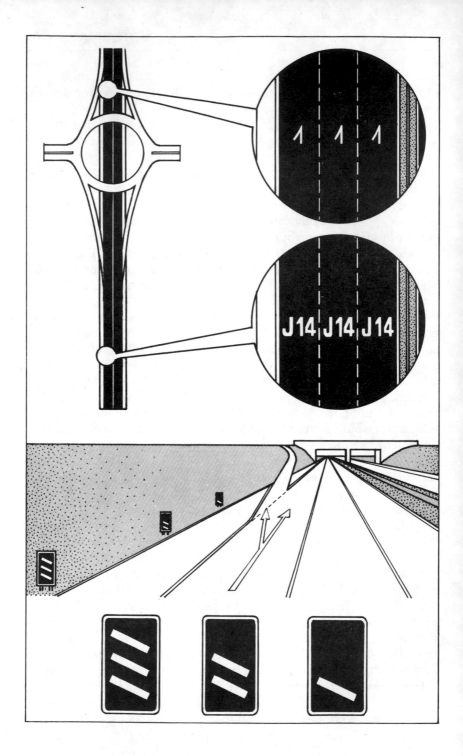

Motorways will soon become a normal part of your driving, and guarding against these hazards will be built into your approach to the task. All that remains is to make sure that the car is as well able to cope as you are. Some modern luxury cars are equipped with cruise control devices, which enable a constant speed to be maintained on motorways and are released by the first touch on the brake pedal. There is no reason, in safety terms, why they should not be used, as long as constant vigilance is maintained – it's all too easy at the best of times to get into a kind of motorway torpor, especially when travelling along with no passenger to chat to – and we can recommend the AE cruise control made as an aftermarket accessory for fitting to existing cars.

No doubt you keep your car in trim, but for a long run on motorways it is worth noting the following points.

To withstand prolonged high speeds, tyres should in many cases be pumped up harder than normal (speed limits being what they are, this is more likely to apply on the Continent than in Britain). The extra air should be added in line with the manufacturer's handbook instructions and when the tyres are still cold before starting the journey. When the tyres have warmed up, the air inside them will show a pressure rise which could lead misguided motorists actually to bleed off some of what appears to be excess pressure. It is very important to keep the correct pressure in the tyre and to avoid overspeeding (a steady 70mph on some heavily loaded low-quality remoulds could be more than they could stand). Analyses of motorway accidents have shown that at least one in six are caused by a tyre failure. Avoid braking violently if you have a puncture at speed. Use gentle brake pressure to reduce the car's speed and steer delicately to avoid starting a skid.

Motorway breakdowns are usually caused by punctures or by driving the vehicle beyond its limitations in age and design. Otherwise they are likely to be the result of simple errors such as running low on petrol and oil.

Left: Carriageway markings on a motorway include a warning that a junction is near (J14 in this case) and, once the junction is passed, a half-chevron indicating that traffic is merging from the left. The distance markers (*below*) are not restricted to motorways, and indicate the distance, in hundreds of yards, to the next point at which a driver may leave a motorway or other route, or a roundabout.

Should you be forced to stop on a motorway (and bear in mind this is permissible only in an emergency), pull onto the hard shoulder. Turn on the hazard warning lights and sidelights to warn other road users, and start walking towards the nearest emergency telephone box. There are red arrows on the marker posts to show you the direction of the nearest one, and the walk cannot be more than about half a mile. Leave any pets in the car, never walk on the motorway itself, and make sure your passengers also stay on the hard shoulder.

20
FOG

Fog should be regarded as a round-the-year hazard in Britain. It is frequently encountered in winter, and encroaches into a significant part of the autumn and spring as well. And there are summer mists which cannot be ignored, too. Of course, the simple solution for successful fog driving is *don't*. But when caught on the road, or if the journey is essential, you have to drive on. However, your main objective should be to avoid dense fog, and bear in mind that an unscheduled overnight stop at a hotel has more appeal than a six months' stint in hospital.

When you do find yourself driving in fog, observe the following rules.

Reduce your speed so that you can stop within your range of vision. This rule applies even if your speed is no higher than 3 or 4mph. You may even be forced to come to a halt and wait for the fog to lift a little. Perhaps you could persuade a passenger to walk in front of the car as a guide. You are asking for trouble if you attempt to drive at anything above this 'braking distance rate': before long you will collide with something. And it is foolhardy to pick up a white line and follow it blindly. You may be lucky and survive for years using this technique, but the time will come when you crash into the back of an unlit, stationary vehicle.

If you decide the fog is so thick you must stop, get off the road. Do your best to ensure that no one is likely to run into the back of you by leaving your lights and hazard warning flashers switched on.

Use the white lines and cats eyes only as a guide, and rely instead on your own eyesight and that of your passengers. Never straddle a white line, as you might meet someone coming the opposite way doing exactly the same thing.

Never use sidelights alone. Keep the headlights on dipped beam: in daylight they will help drivers approaching from the opposite direction to see you much earlier than if your sidelights are the only warning. Use the dipped beam at night, as this reflects back much less light into your eyes than a main beam. It is possible that at night you *may* find it easier not to use headlights, but do bear in mind that it is as important to be seen as to see.

The rule at junctions is to flash the lights and sound your horn, then lower your window and listen for other vehicles approaching. When turning right, you must exercise special care as an approaching driver may not be expecting someone to emerge from the fog in front.

In fog, it is easy to get the impression that the vehicle in front is moving unnecessarily slowly, and it's possible you will be foolish enough to overtake. *Don't.* Overtaking in fog not only invites a head-on collision with approaching vehicles, but it is often the result of being misled. The vehicle in front makes a 'hole' in the droplets of water vapour that form fog. As you catch up, you pass into a relatively clear space and assume that the fog has eased a little. You pull out to pass and then realise that the fog is as thick as ever and you are forced to continue a highly dangerous manoeuvre with near-zero visibility.

It is prudent to stay in line, therefore, but take care not to follow a driver whose speed you judge to be too fast for safety. And if you are following a vehicle, make sure there is sufficient space in which to stop if necessary. That space allowance should not be based on the assumption that the driver will brake to a halt in the normal way. There is always the risk that the leader of a convoy may collide with a crashed car, and this is more likely to happen in fog. This is, unfortunately, a familiar occurrence on motorways (the so-called concertina crash), despite the constant pleas from police and road safety officers for more care. Because the leader is heading a nose-to-tail convoy, the result is another major, multi-vehicle pile-up.

It's really no surprise that motorways achieve maximum publicity when there are fog crashes. If only drivers would follow the rules outlined here, rather than driving on blindly at high speed, there is no reason why motorways should not be safer than any other type of road (as they are under normal weather conditions). Motorway police warning signals and radio broadcasts offer some guidance, and the dangers of fog can be reduced (though not eliminated) if you know what to expect. Perhaps CB radio will help. There is also your own judgement of the weather and how it is likely to develop in the next few hours.

Mist, however, can loom up when you least expect it. An undulating country main road can harbour pockets of mist in the valleys even in midsummer if the humidity, temperature and air currents are right. Sometimes, in other weather conditions, the valleys are clear and the hilltops shrouded. If you are travelling at 60mph or so and hit a patch of mist, you have little time to slow down. Take all the usual precautions when mist does appear. Drop your speed and bring the lights into play, including the auxiliary foglamps if your car has them. If you use foglamps, there must be two in operation unless the headlights are also switched on. This law is intended to ensure that other drivers do not mistake your vehicle for a motorcycle.

Switch on the windscreen wipers as well. Though some fogs appear to be quite 'dry', others are very moist and the vapour quickly condenses on the windscreen to reduce your visibility still further unless the wipers are working. Use the washer from time to time. The windows should be kept open a little if this helps to reduce condensation inside the car, and leave the ventilation running in the demist position to keep the inside of the windscreen clear. Turn on the rear window heater if one is fitted.

21

ACCIDENTS

Hopefully, you will never be involved in an accident, although statistically the chance of avoiding one throughout your motoring career is small – even for advanced drivers. Even then, you can be pretty sure that sooner or later you will come upon the scene of one. Indeed, you may be among the first to arrive, and it will then be your responsibility to lend a helping hand. This is the expert's advice, from the Metropolitan Police, on what to do.

Stop and think
At a road accident there are many things that have to be done at once, and there is more involved than merely helping the casualties. Warn other drivers, send for help, and protect the site from further accidents until the emergency services arrive. What you do in those first few minutes could be a matter of life or death. For instance, would you run to the casualties and start to pull them out? If you did, you would be wrong.

Park safely
Do not park your vehicle where it could become a hazard to other traffic. Park at the roadside between the accident site and oncoming traffic where your car can easily be seen. Keep any children inside the car. At night, park so that you can light the accident with your headlamps and still be seen by oncoming traffic. Switch on your hazard warning lights if fitted. Switch off the crashed vehicle's engine and apply the hand brake. If necessary, chock the wheels and disconnect the car battery. Warn bystanders to stop smoking at or near the scene. Keep your fire extinguisher handy.

Warn other road users
Oncoming drivers need plenty of time and distance in which to

understand warning signals and to slow down and stop or negotiate the accident. Do not run or stand in the road waving wildly. You will confuse others and put yourself in peril. Walk back on the kerb or verge for at least 100 yards, or until the accident is going out of view. Give the 'slow down' signal clearly and point definitely to the accident scene. On bends, a second person may be needed for advance warning.

Get someone to stand near the site and guide vehicles round the accident. At night, stand under a streetlamp or in the headlights of a car. Hold a white handkerchief or, better still, a torch in your signalling hand. It will help if you wear a pale coat or shirt or something reflective. If you carry an advance warning sign (a red reflecting triangle), place it in the road to warn approaching traffic of an obstruction. The sign should be placed at least 50 yards (150 yards on motorways) before the accident scene and on the same side of the road.

Send for help
Your first priority is to send for help, because you will need it! Don't leave casualties unattended – send someone to telephone for help. However, if there is nobody around, you must go yourself.

Answer these questions at the accident scene
What is the *exact* location? (If you don't know, and there are no road signs, look for an obvious landmark). How many casualties are there? Is the accident causing danger? Is other traffic jamming up? Are petrol or chemicals spilling? Are the casualties trapped? How many vehicles are involved? Are they cars? Lorries? Tankers? Buses or coaches?

Dial 999
Tell the operator your telephone number and ask for ambulance, police or fire brigade, and you will be connected to each in turn. Ask for:

Ambulance   if there are casualties.

Police   if there are casualties, danger, or obstruction to traffic.

Fire brigade   if there are people trapped, petrol or chemicals on the road, or risk of fire.

Give this information

Exact location of the accident; number and general condition of casualties; if anyone is trapped; number and type of vehicles involved; if petrol or chemicals are on the road; if other traffic is in danger or jamming up; your name, address, and telephone number from which you are speaking.

Return to the scene of the accident to help with the casualties or traffic. If you saw what happened, give your name and address to the attending police officer. If you have to leave the accident scene before speaking to the police, please contact any police station or officer as soon as possible to give details.

If an accident involving only slight damage to vehicles and committing no offence occurs, it is not necessary to report it. Those involved are, however, legally bound to exchange details of driver, owner, and vehicle registration number. If injury is caused you must also give your insurance particulars. If anyone requires advice or assistance, telephone the local police station. If urgent, use the 999 system.

Help the casualties

Don't move injured people unless there is immediate danger. You could aggravate internal and back or neck injuries. Make sure the person can breathe. Inspect the inside of the mouth and back of the throat. Remove any food, sweets, or false teeth, on which they might choke. Listen, and if you cannot detect breathing, try to restore the casualty by mouth-to-mouth resuscitation.

Place the casualty on his back. Support the neck so that the head falls back to open the airway. Pinch his nose shut and hold his mouth open. Cover his mouth with yours, and blow out firmly to inflate his lungs. Then release nose and mouth. Keep repeating until the casualty starts breathing spontaneously. If the casualty is unconscious, move him gently into the recovery position to make sure he does not choke on his tongue or gorge. This involves turning the casualty gently on his side and bending the arms and legs as shown so as to keep him in position. Straighten and turn his head to one side, facing slightly downwards.

To stop serious bleeding apply very firm pressure to the bleeding point to stem the flow of blood. Use a pad or apply a sterile dressing and bandage firmly. Look for fractures of the limbs, and try to stop those limbs moving. If casualties are still sitting up and in no

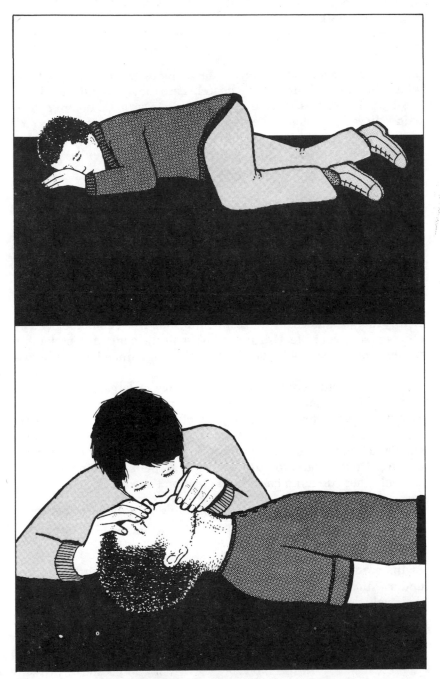

The recovery position (*top*) and the kiss of life. Their application is described on the facing page.

immediate danger, do not make them leave the car. Leave them where they are and support the head in case they pass out and choke.

Keep all casualties, including shock cases, warm. Do not give them pain relievers, alcohol, other drinks, food or cigarettes – they may have internal injuries and need operations.

If you're not sure what to do, leave well alone, provided they are breathing and not bleeding heavily.

Get first aid training

This chapter gives only the most elementary first aid advice. If you have been trained in first aid you will obviously be able to do more and better than this. The British Red Cross Society or the St John Ambulance Association will advise you about training.

Carry a first aid kit

Be prepared to help yourself and other road users. Always carry a clearly marked and easily accessible first aid kit – it could be used by others to save your life. Use any suitable plastic container, preferably flexible and transparent. Mark it 'First Aid' or paint a large red cross on it.

This box should contain sterile dressings in large, medium, and small sizes – as many as you can fit in. Triangular bandages for use as slings or bandages, and safety pins, plasters, scissors and knife are essential. Although not to be used in accidents, you could carry anti-sting and scald ointments for minor mishaps that might impair your driving. Do not carry or use antiseptics, pain relieving pills, or alcohol. These do more harm than good on the road.

(*The Institute's thanks go to the Metropolitan Police for the above advice.*)

Fire

At the scene of the accident, there is just one set of circumstances under which you should break the rule and get injured people out of their vehicles. Fire is an unlikely but none the less serious hazard which occurs in only a minute percentage of all accidents, but when it *does* happen then immediate action and presence of mind are essential. The fire may be an electrical one, caused by a short circuit from damaged wiring. As long as petrol is not leaking out of a ruptured tank dangerously near it, you should have plenty of time to deal with the matter. If your own car carries a fire extinguisher (ideally, a 3lb-plus BCF model and not one of the almost useless very small extinguishers), then aim it at the base of the flames and keep up the discharge until the fire is out.

The fire may be under the bonnet, however, in which case care is needed since the action of opening the bonnet will feed the fire with huge draughts of air, enabling it to flare up. If you can do so, open the bonnet just a fraction, aiming the extinguisher inside, *but only if you can positively identify the source of the flames.* If you can't, then open the bonnet wide and be prepared to act quickly if the fire expands. At the same time, try to disconnect one of the battery leads in order to break the electrical circuit that is feeding the fire.

A petrol fire is another matter, calling for heroics of a high order if anything is to be done to help those involved. Remember, though, that most petrol fires can be avoided by extreme care to ensure that no one smokes, walks in nailed shoes, or tries to cut away damaged metal in the vicinity. Fuel leaking out onto the road or into the car can be easily ignited by a spark (so switch off the car's ignition) but petrol certainly won't set itself alight.

Accident procedures
Fire is usually a part of the most serious kind of accident, whereas the majority of accidents are no more than bumps, scrapes and very minor collisions. Even these should be treated seriously, of course, and in any event it would be highly unethical, not to say illegal, to damage a parked car by brushing against its wing and then drive off without leaving a note with your name and address under the windscreen wiper.

In a more serious collision, the law *demands* that you give your name, address, and insurance company's name and address to the other driver and to anyone else, such as a police officer, who may reasonably require it. You in turn should ensure that you get the relevant names and addresses from the other party. Make sure, too, that you collect information from anyone – whether motorist or pedestrian – who happened to be around at the time and be quick about it. Witnesses, not wanting to spend a day in court on your behalf, have a habit of vanishing as soon as the dust settles.

If all these points have been complied with, then you are not required by law to contact the police. However, it is always advisable to do so if someone has been injured or when there is an allegation of dangerous driving.

If the crash is anything more than a minor affair, leave the vehicles involved where they came to rest. If you happen to be carrying a camera take photographs of your own – they may prove very useful indeed if the matter ever comes before a court. The police will want to take measurements – this, of course, being the prime reason for leaving the vehicles unmoved – but you could do so as well since your insurance company will probably want to know exactly what happened.

The more precise the information you can give your insurers, the better are their chances of making certain that, if the other driver was to blame, it is his company and not yours that pays up.

After an accident, be careful not to say anything, either to the other driver or to the police, that you may regret later. Quite apart from anything else, your natural sense of relief may make your tongue wag enough to say things that may subsequently be misinterpreted as acceptance by you of liability. Even if you feel the fault was yours, think deeply before you speak. Some insurance companies have even been known to put a clause in the policy removing their liability to any client who accepts the blame, or even just apologises, in post-accident conversation.

Of course, the collision may be a very minor one with no more than superficial damage to one or both cars. In circumstances like these, however aggrieved you may feel, the best advice today seems to be 'grin and bear it'. If the road is at all busy, other motorists won't thank you for causing a traffic jam while you sort out a matter of a dented bumper. The police won't thank you either for dragging them into a matter likely to be so inconsequential as not to merit prosecution.

You are unlikely to be able to make the other person's insurance company pay up, simply because they know that the cost, time and trouble of legal action will more than outweigh anything you might recover, and you will hardly want to go to your own insurer with a claim which will be a black mark on your record *and* is probably worth no more than a year or two of the no-claims bonus you would lose. So in this day and age, however annoying it might be at the time, it's best to put these minor knocks down to experience. Strictly speaking, however, you should notify *all* accidents to the insurers. You may head the report 'For information only at the moment'.

If you witness a 'hit and run' accident, try to obtain and write down the registration number, make and colour of the vehicle involved, together with as many relevant details as possible to assist the police to identify the car. If you can get a description of the driver, so much the better. Pass any details obtained to the police as soon as practicable, but don't forget that your first duty is to any injured victims.

22
REACTION TIMES

A car travels a long way while its driver is simply reacting to a situation, as we have seen in Chapter 6 – and that distance is covered before the driver has even started to do anything about it.

Naturally, reaction times vary widely. A professional racing driver, experienced in high speed driving and drawing on reserves of nervous energy, may produce remarkable times: perhaps as low as 0·2 of a second. This represents the time which elapses between the driver spotting a hazard ahead of him and his foot beginning to press the brake pedal or his hand moving the steering wheel. When you consider that it takes about one second to say 'one thousand', and that our man has recognised the danger, decided on its potential, considered what may happen next, chosen a course of action, and acted in a fifth of that time, you realise that his reactions are exceptionally fast.

For the average motorist, reaction times are much slower. Around 0·5 of a second is still good, 0·8 fair and even a whole second not too bad (longer than one second is beginning to get dangerously slow). It is difficult to test your own time unless you have access to a proper medically-overseen check. There is a parlour game in which you have to grip a long card that someone drops between your thumb and finger, but that is hardly an accurate guide. Simulation testers at some driving centres are much better. You sit at the simulated controls of a car and a hazard or sometimes just a simple 'brake' warning flashes up on a screen in front of you.

Remember that the speed of your own reactions will apply only in the context of when it is measured. If you are tired, ill, or even just emotionally distressed your reactions will slow down. This must be taken into account and your driving must be modified accordingly if you have to drive when you are feeling below par in this way. In good health, your reaction time may be 0·5 seconds, but when you

The tables *below* show how far you travel in feet during every tenth of a second while reacting – and before operating the brakes or steering – for a quick reaction time of 0.4 seconds.

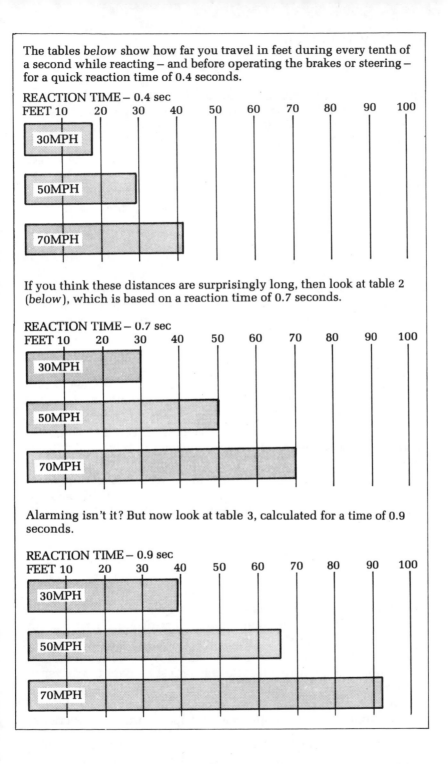

REACTION TIME – 0.4 sec

If you think these distances are surprisingly long, then look at table 2 (*below*), which is based on a reaction time of 0.7 seconds.

REACTION TIME – 0.7 sec

Alarming isn't it? But now look at table 3, calculated for a time of 0.9 seconds.

REACTION TIME – 0.9 sec

have a heavy cold it can increase to 0·8 seconds. Those extra three-tenths of a second can make a tremendous difference in terms of the distance travelled before you start to take action to avoid a hazard ahead.

Now you can see how far you can travel, while you merely react to a hazard, if your reaction time is a reasonable 0·9 seconds. It is important, therefore, always to allow for this in the semi-instinctive calculations we all have to make on the road: braking distances, overtaking and so on.

By reading the road ahead and realising that a hazard might occur at any moment, it is possible to reduce the distance a little. If you have reason to believe a hazard is developing ahead, it is wise to lift off the accelerator and hold your right foot poised over the brake, ready to apply it if the need arises. In this way you will have saved the time necessary for the brain to send a 'lift off the throttle, move onto the brake' message to your foot. And that might save some of those invaluable tenths of a second.

Because your eyes need to adjust to the changing conditions of light and dark, you will need more time in which to react at night. This is because the iris quickly closes down to adjust your vision when bright headlights approach, but it takes much longer to adjust to darkness again when the lights have passed. You are driving with temporarily defective vision while your eyes grow accustomed to the dark again. This makes it harder to see what lies ahead and so increases the time needed in which to recognise developments that may affect you. Your reaction time can rise to several seconds at such a time, as you will find in Chapter 12. Allow for this and adjust your speed accordingly.

While we can take a little positive action to recognise the effects of reaction time in ourselves, there is nothing to be done about the shortcomings of those around us. All too frequently someone involved in an accident complains that the other driver 'had plenty of time to see me', and by his standards maybe he did. The trouble is, it may not have been enough for the other driver. The smash was caused by Driver One assuming that Driver Two's reactions were quicker than they were, and that his manoeuvre would be completed safely. Much of the blame for the crash must lie with the driver who thought, wrongly, that the other 'had plenty of time to see me'.

Before leaving reaction times, there are a couple of myths which must be exploded. One is that alcohol speeds up your reactions. In fact, it has exactly the opposite effect because it depresses the nervous system, so you react more slowly to outside influences. The problem is that people often *think* they react more quickly after a few drinks, and this can be traced back to the sense of excitement and heightened awareness that is produced by drinking alcohol. The rule is familiar but still essential: don't drink and drive. Remember too that drugs can also slow you down and, if your doctor prescribes any drug, check with him that it is safe for you to drive. For the same reason, read the labels on proprietary pills you buy from the chemist. Anti-sickness tablets are just one of the examples of drugs which can have disastrous side-effects if you are driving.

Let us also dispose of another favourite claim – 'I stopped dead' – after spotting a hazard ahead. Take a few moments to consider how far you travel while reacting and you will see this cannot be true. And, in any case, stopping 'dead' is totally beyond the capabilities of every car, quite apart from the fact that instant deceleration would kill the occupants.

23

IN GEAR

The skilled driver will know how to get the most out of his car when the occasion demands, as we have already seen. But it is not sufficient to know the rate of acceleration when the pedal is depressed: we must also fully appreciate the proper use of the gearbox. The majority of cars still have a manual gearbox with four or five forward gears, and we will examine these first, while recognising that an increasing number of drivers opt for automatic transmission.

It is essential to be completely familiar with the box, so that you can make any gear selection quickly and accurately. The advanced test calls for an ability to go up and down through the ratios and, although today's all-synchromesh gearboxes reduce the problems, a degree of skill is still necessary. Nowadays, double de-clutching is usually not necessary.

When changing up a gear, you should release the accelerator completely and depress it again only when the clutch has been re-engaged. On a downward change, though, rev up as you select the lower gear so that the engine speed is matched to road speed as the drive takes up again. You will find this minimises any strain on the transmission and will also give a smooth gearchange. When executed with finesse, the gearchange should not be noticed by your passengers.

While we are apt to disregard double de-clutching these days, there are still a few cars on the road with non-synchromesh bottom gears. The synchromesh mechanism, now almost universal in car transmission, relieves the driver of the need to double de-clutch. But it is as well to know how to cope if you come across a non-synchro bottom gear and have to double de-clutch. If you want to change up to a higher gear, depress the clutch pedal and release the accelerator, move the gear lever into neutral, let up the clutch for a moment and then push it down again and engage the gear.

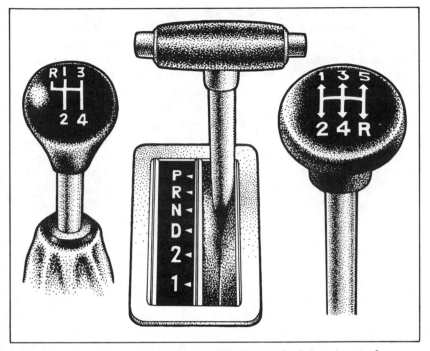

Some common types of gear selection levers. On the *left* is a typical gear lever for a four-speed manually operated gearbox. On the *right* is its five-speed counterpart. The central stick is typical of many automatics, and the letters indicate parking lock (P), which locks the transmission when the car is stationary (a useful adjunct to the handbrake); reverse (R); neutral (N) – note that you must usually select P or N in order to allow the engine to be started; forward drive (D) – this can be selected and left alone for most purposes; and low gears (1 or 2), which are for holding the car in that particular gear.

When changing down, depress the clutch pedal, move the gear lever into neutral, bring up the clutch pedal and rev the engine to synchronise the relevant speeds. Then depress the clutch again and engage the gear. You will soon get the feel of the engine speed necessary when you have practised for a while, and will also be able to co-ordinate the other operations which seem so daunting at first, yet become easy when you know how – a premise which applies to so many aspects of good driving.

Double de-clutching techniques can be used with a modern gearbox, but you will gain nothing because the designers have installed synchromesh to do the job for you.

Correct use of the gears is one of the basics of advanced driving. You should always start from rest in first gear, even if the car will manage it in second. Starting in second wears out the clutch, since you have to engage it much more slowly and let it slip more. This reduces your initial rate of acceleration and increases the risk of stalling if you are not careful.

Make sure you are familiar with the maximum speeds attainable in the intermediate gears. These are usually to be found in the manufacturer's manual, and are sometimes marked on the speedometer. While overtaking, never hesitate to take the car to these speeds if it is necessary but, equally, it is wrong to extend the engine beyond those limits. And do not attempt to change down to a lower ratio while driving at more than the maximum recommended for that gear.

A rev-counter is a useful aid, and it is possible to fit one if your car is not already equipped. This instrument shows the engine speed in revolutions per minute and you can mark on it the maximum safe figures. You can make sure you never over-rev the engine by keeping an eye on the dial. The rev-counter is also a useful guide to ensuring that you don't rev too slowly. Few engines perform well under 2000rpm, and you should keep them running above that speed for the smoothest performance. You will soon know when the engine is beginning to labour (running in too high a gear) from the sound it makes, but the rev-counter acts as a useful source of auxiliary information.

Some motorists seem determined to keep a car in top gear for as long as possible when it is moving. Don't do that; the intermediate ratios are there to be used, for hills, overtaking, and at other times. It is more sensible to make the fullest use of the facilities provided by the manufacturer. At the same time, it is wrong to change gear too often. Engines these days have considerable flexibility but it is wrong to allow them to labour or to keep working away at high revs. You should not use the gears to slow the car down, unless you have to contend with brake failure. This job should be done by the brakes, and the correct procedure is to change down as the speed drops.

An automatic transmission overcomes these problems because it thinks for itself. Most can be left with the selector lever in position D (for drive) or its equivalent. They will change up and down fully automatically as well as providing the clutch action to move you

The tachometer or rev-counter is a useful instrument. Many cars don't carry them as standard, but you can easily get one fitted. It not only gives an over-revving check, but also indicates when you may be labouring the engine, and you can also work out the maximum number of revolutions per minute for each gear, thus giving you a valuable insight into your car's performance potential in possibly dangerous situations like overtaking.

away from stationary and to free the drive when the car stops again. There are times when the driver's judgement is superior to that of the automatic transmission and most gearboxes of this type have an overriding control. It is often better to control the gear selection yourself if you want maximum acceleration or to move a heavy load from rest on a hill.

The Automotive Products type of gearbox gives the driver full control over the four forward ratios should he demand it. The transmission then functions like an ordinary manual gearbox but still has automatic clutch action. If the gears are left to change themselves, the driver will possibly notice a small loss in performance.

The widely used Borg Warner automatic transmission, and some others, may have only three forward gears and there may be less opportunity to operate override. However, they can be kept in the lower ratios when full acceleration is needed by moving the selector lever to an intermediate position by pressing the accelerator to the floor.

Other types of automatic transmission tend to follow one of these basic patterns, with the exception of the system developed by Daf of Holland, which was later used on smaller Volvos. With this transmission there are no gears as such, but instead it relies on steel-reinforced flexible belts running over pulleys to provide an infinitely variable range of ratios. The only control needed on the Daf and Volvo is a lever to select forward and reverse, apart from a switch on the facia which brings in extra engine braking effect for long descents.

The gearbox should never be used in place of the brakes, but it can be a useful aid when slowing down. Remember, however, that engine braking with an automatic is less effective than with a manual. If you have become accustomed to a manual gearbox, an automatic will seem strange at first. If you passed the driving test in recent years in a car fitted with automatic transmission, you will be restricted to driving cars of that type. You will have to take another test in a car fitted with a manual gearbox to obtain a full licence which allows you to drive vehicles of that sort.

It is a point worth noting that some automatics can be damaged if the car is towed after a breakdown. Always check in the manufacturer's handbook that towing is in order.

24

SYMPATHY AND UNDERSTANDING

A reasonable awareness of what is happening under the bonnet as you drive and make various demands on your car will help you to develop a greater appreciation of your vehicle. If you treat it properly, it will serve you better. After all, the car is a machine constructed to take you from one place to another and you, as the operator, will not be able to do the best possible job unless you have at least an idea of how that machine works. This is not the place to explore the subject in great detail – there are many excellent handbooks which already cover that area in depth for everyone from the qualified engineer to the interested layman. But you may find a brief description helpful.

Let's start with the engine, which burns petrol (or possibly diesel) with a mixture of air to create an expansion of gas that drives the pistons. These pistons in turn drive a rotating shaft. (In rotary engines the end result – a fast-turning shaft – is achieved by a rotor instead of pistons.) The shaft is connected to the gearbox by a clutch which can be released to allow the engine to run when the car is standing still.

There are various combinations of gearwheels inside the gearbox, which give the various ratios as they are selected by the driver. They are necessary because it is important to keep the engine turning within its comfortable speed range (normally about 2000rpm as a minimum up to a maximum of about 6000rpm) regardless of road speed. So you start in a low gear and change up as the speed increases. Articulated shafts take the power from the gearbox to the driven wheels, which may be at the front or back (or both).

The wheels are attached to the car by pivoted arms and occasionally by the springs themselves. When the springs do not provide this wheel locating function, they are usually of the coil type. The springs are there to insulate the car and its occupants from bumps and hollows in the road surface, and also to ensure that the tyres remain

The basic workings of a typical modern car.

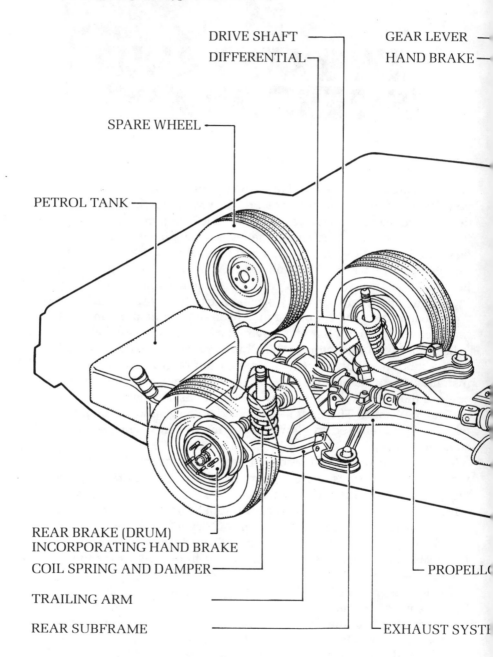

DRIVE SHAFT

DIFFERENTIAL

GEAR LEVER —

HAND BRAKE—

SPARE WHEEL

PETROL TANK

REAR BRAKE (DRUM)
INCORPORATING HAND BRAKE

COIL SPRING AND DAMPER

TRAILING ARM

REAR SUBFRAME

PROPELL

EXHAUST SYST

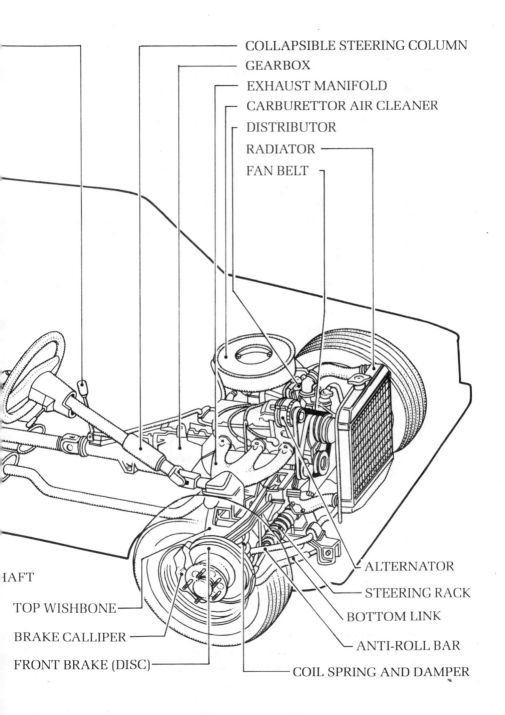

COLLAPSIBLE STEERING COLUMN

GEARBOX

EXHAUST MANIFOLD

CARBURETTOR AIR CLEANER

DISTRIBUTOR

RADIATOR

FAN BELT

ALTERNATOR

STEERING RACK

BOTTOM LINK

ANTI-ROLL BAR

HAFT

TOP WISHBONE

BRAKE CALLIPER

FRONT BRAKE (DISC)

COIL SPRING AND DAMPER

firmly in contact with the road. Clearly, a wheel that has bounced into the air after hitting a ridge will contribute nothing to the car's steering or braking until it comes down onto the road again.

Whether the brakes are of the disc or drum variety, the principle does not change: a lining of special high-friction material is forced into contact with the disc or drum attached to the wheel to slow its rotation.

Those with a deeper understanding of car mechanisms will hopefully forgive this brief appraisal, for it may help some people to have a better understanding of this complicated piece of machinery.

No one would reasonably expect the engine with a working speed of between 2000 and 6000rpm to perform satisfactorily if top speed was engaged at around 1500rpm. Likewise, you are heading for trouble if you constantly rev it beyond the limits of safety. The advanced driver, being skilled, will ensure that the power unit is running comfortably, probably on part throttle once he has reached the required cruising speed. It is quite wrong to drive unnecessarily quickly and be forced to jam on the brakes at every obstacle. Try to drive at a 'happy balance' speed at all times, and remember it is always better to err on the slow side rather than the fast.

Next, the clutch. This is responsible for transmitting the engine's power to the gearbox, and is comprised of two facing discs that can be brought together to engage the drive or pushed apart to release it. The grip is provided by a lining of friction material, so you will see that, if you slip the clutch (i.e. press the pedal just enough to hold the two discs only partially engaged), you will wear out the friction lining quickly, not to mention expensively. A clutch will serve you for tens of thousands of miles if it is treated with respect, yet a driver with no mechanical sympathy may wear one out after only 5000 miles. As far as the clutch is concerned, the worst sin is driving with the left foot continually on the pedal. Many motorists who slip into this habit think the slight pressure of a foot just resting on the pedal is insufficient to cause any harm. It is, however, just enough to let the clutch slip a little all the time, which wears it out quickly.

Another fault – and one which often develops without the driver even realising it – is to use the clutch pedal to control the speed of the car. This is done by dipping the clutch while negotiating a tight corner, then feeding it in again gently when lining up for the next stretch of straight road. The theory is that this avoids changing down a gear but the effect is to wear out the clutch and to leave the driver in the wrong gear for the conditions. It is also wrong to hold the car on a hill, waiting to re-start, by keeping the clutch partially engaged and revving the engine. The hand brake is there for use on such occasions.

Slipping the clutch means that it is used too gently, but it is also possible to be too sharp with it. A 'jack rabbit' start places a heavy, if brief, strain on the whole transmission system as well as the engine. This violent engagement of the clutch can break gears in the transmission if repeated often enough. It also wears out the tyres and damages the universal joints in the drive shafts, the latter fault being identified by a loud 'clonk' every time you change gear.

The gearbox comes next. Make sure that the clutch is always fully disengaged before changing gear, and check that the lever is fully pushed home when you select the next ratio.

Everything on your car benefits from careful treatment, including the brakes. In addition to being risky, leaving your braking to the last moment also wears out the friction lining much more quickly.

25
TOWING

These days, so many people tow trailers of one kind or another –
whether caravans, or trailers for the transportation of boats, horses or
whatever – that a separate towing test has been introduced by the
Institute of Advanced Motorists. It is open only to existing members
who have already passed the advanced test in a car or commercial
vehicle.

The basic points to bear in mind when towing a trailer are as
follows:

Keep the nose weight fairly high but not excessive – a downward
pressure of anything from 50 to 150lb on the car's towbar is usually
needed to ensure stability.

Always double-check that the towball is fully latched home, that
safety chains and emergency brake pulls are in position and that all
the trailer lights are working.

Ensure that the load, whatever it may be, is secured.

Check tyre pressures. Those in the rear tyres of the tow vehicle
may need to be increased, and the pressure of the trailer tyres
themselves must be right – which often calls for a much higher
pressure than for the tow vehicle's tyres.

Release the parking brake and any overrun brake catch on the
drawbar.

Braking
Even with overrun brakes you will find that stopping distances are
increased considerably; after all, the trailer when laden could weigh
a ton or more and that means a lot of momentum.

In traffic
It is most important to allow for the extra width of the trailer, and to
remember that, when negotiating junctions, the trailer will cut in

closer to the kerb than the car itself. So make a larger arc of the corner, if it is safe to do so, or emulate the drivers of articulated lorries by drawing slightly past the apex with the 'tractor unit', in this case your car, then turn in abruptly.

Rear vision
Accessory shops sell wing mirrors on extended arms that are well nigh essential for adequate rearward vision if you are towing anything other than a flat trailer.

Legal requirements
The speed limits which apply to trailers vary considerably, according to the road and to the design of the trailer. So do weight restrictions, these being related to the weight of the towing vehicle. In addition, there are requirements governing lights, rear reflectors and the display of 50mph limit warning signs at the rear. The law is too complex for us to go into detail here, but you can check it either with the company that supplies your trailer or by asking the local police.

Although not always a legal requirement, we would recommend that you fit sidelights halfway along the trailer on the mudguards, showing red to the rear and white ahead. It's surprising how many other road users fail to spot a trailer, especially if it's unladen, and this precaution could help prevent an accident.

Manoeuvring
This, as the saying goes, is what sorts the men from the boys as far as trailers are concerned. Reversing is the most tricky, and we would advise plenty of practice – perhaps in a public car park on a Sunday morning – before you have to do it for real. The basic point to bear in mind is that a trailer will normally travel in the opposite direction to the way in which the car is heading. That is, if you back around to the left the trailer will swing to the right. So to make the trailer move to the left, you have to start by backing to the right, then correcting and backing left as the trailer assumes the required direction of travel. It takes time to master the technique but, as with riding a bicycle, when you have acquired the knack it will seem quite easy. Take care, however, not to have so much steering lock on the car that the trailer jack-knifes and becomes wedged against the rear bumper. Back gently, if necessary edging forward and having another go, until you get it right.

Don't forget that on many trailers the overrun brakes have to be latched out of use if they are not to clamp on as soon as you reverse.

Finally, on the open road, be prepared for the dreaded swing, in which at a certain speed the trailer will start to oscillate astern, building up bigger and bigger swings until it threatens to send the whole rig lurching off the road. The short-term cure is to slow down, but do this gently or else the already unsteady trailer will launch into even more violent action. The real answer is to reload the trailer itself so that more weight presses down on the drawbar.

26

DRIVING ABROAD

There is nothing to prevent a reasonably competent driver taking his car abroad on holiday, and soon feeling perfectly confident when driving around. There are great pleasures in store once you cross the Channel and reach the Continent. Away from the trunk roads and crowded autoroutes and autobahns, it is easy to find pleasing highways which have much less traffic than that usually found in our compact country. And there is no reason to fear driving through cities like Paris or Rome – despite their awesome reputation for reckless drivers – as long as you observe the basic rules of advanced motoring.

As with every other aspect of advanced driving, you must plan ahead. For this task the planning starts at home and, when you have decided upon your destination, go out and buy large-scale road maps (the Michelin series sold by most bookshops are among the best). When planning a route, you will be forced to choose the motorways if you are in a hurry. But if you have time to make a more leisurely journey, draw a straight line in pencil between the ferry arrival port and your final destination. Then ink in a route along whichever roads – be they primary or secondary – run closest to your pencil line. This will call for some navigational skill on the part of your passenger but that can be part of the enjoyment of the holiday, and will prevent boredom. This method is not likely to be the quickest way of reaching your destination, but it does provide a delightful way to see more of the country. The quiet rural roads are much more relaxing than the major routes which carry commercial traffic, and the scenery will be more attractive for your passengers.

In addition to the maps, you will need guide books to tell you about the main areas of interest and where to stay. Many people make the mistake of buying too many and may be surprised to learn how much material is available free on request from the state tourist offices of the countries you will be passing through. Nearly all of these offices have branches in London.

Members of the AA and RAC can make all the travelling arrangements through their organisation, including car insurance to make sure of your vehicle's return to Britain in the event of a major breakdown. Don't forget to take out insurance for your own health and against all other possibilities – no matter how remote they may appear. As far as the car is concerned, you must tell your broker, agent or insurance company where and when you are going. You do not legally need any extra cover when driving in other Common Market countries, but the basic insurance provided automatically is the bare minimum. To rely upon this alone would almost certainly leave you with substantial bills in the event of trouble abroad. So be prepared to pay more and get full cover for the Continent, rather than settling for the inadequate minimum.

It is possible to arrange other details of travel preparation yourself, or they can be handled by a local travel agent. You can choose to cross the Channel either by hovercraft or by boat. Some people choose the hovercraft because it is the quickest and most exciting, but it is also rather noisy and is sometimes kept in port by weather which does not prevent other ferries from operating.

Few moments can compare with the one when you drive off the ferry and into another country. At first you will probably remind yourself constantly to 'keep right' and for the first few miles this will ensure that you drive on the 'wrong' side of the road without mishap. The trouble comes later when you have gained some experience and begin to feel more confident. It is at this point that you could forget the rule of staying on the 'wrong' side of the highway, a fact borne out by the statistics which show that most accidents involving British cars happen within a hundred miles of the Channel ports. The time to be on your guard is after a halt when you have parked your car on the left-hand side of the road. It seems quite natural to come out of the shop or garage, get in the car and drive up the road . . . on the left.

Apart from this aspect of driving abroad, most Continental traffic rules are much the same as British ones. There is one important exception, which we will look at in a moment. Traffic signs do not present a problem, as they follow an international pattern already familiar in Britain. You can interpret the few local peculiarities by using a little imagination and a lot of common sense. One of the more bizarre signs, found in some areas of France, is a silhouette of a frog inside a red triangle which tells you that, at certain times of the year, there will be so many frogs on the road that it will become slippery.

Beware the traffic lights which authorities sometimes suspend from overhead cables or attach to the sides of houses. They can be hard to spot. Far more traffic lights have filters than in Britain (for left, right and/or straight on), and the amber intermediate stage is sometimes omitted.

The important exception to British traffic rules mentioned above is the well known 'priority to the right' rule, seen at its most virulent in France. It means what it says: you must give way to traffic coming from the right. It is confusing to British drivers because it includes vehicles coming out of side roads or any seemingly unimportant road on the right. On a roundabout the rule means you must yield to traffic entering it from the outside: watch out for this, because it is the exact opposite of the rule in Britain. There are other exceptions, too, so do check with the touring organisations.

An exception to the 'priority to the right' rule occurs when you are on a main road and a sign of a broad main route crossed by a thinner minor one shows that you have right of way in that case. But take care, because even this is applied inconsistently. At the next junction there may be a crossroads sign indicating that you now have to give way to traffic from the right. Priority applies automatically in towns, no matter how major your road and how minor the one joining it. It would be reasonable to assume that local drivers would use this curious rule with some care, but many don't. Look out for the driver who hurtles into your path without pausing to look up the road to check whether you can slow down or steer clear. It will come as no surprise when you learn that France, which greatly favours the priority rule, has one of the highest accident rates in Europe. You have been warned.

In addition to this warning, there are a few more aspects of European driving over which you must take especial care. These are mentioned in the hope that they will enable you to enjoy your Continental touring holiday, and not with the aim of putting you off it altogether.

The first point to note is that Continental policemen, particularly the motorcycle police in France, operate in a much harsher way towards motorists than their counterparts in Britain. They are known to lurk behind bushes at spots where drivers tend to slow rather than stop for a Halt sign. They will listen to no excuses and more often than not impose an on-the-spot fine, even if the driver concerned was not taking a risk and there was no other traffic about. A French policeman even has the power, in some circumstances, to ban you from driving there and then. Admittedly, we do not know of a Briton who has suffered this penalty and have heard of only a few cases in which drivers have been fined abroad for anything other than a parking offence. But bear in mind that Continental police do take a tough line and they will not regard ignorance of the law as an excuse.

Another point to watch is that you may have difficulty in finding high grade petrol in many parts of the Continent. If your car is happy with lower or medium grades, there is no problem. But if your engine will take only the best, it is as well to tell your garage before you go. They should be able to adjust the power unit to run properly on cheaper fuel.

The yellow headlights you will encounter in France are required by law there. Visitors are allowed to use their ordinary white lights, but don't be surprised if you get one or two flashes from oncoming motorists at night. However, have the dipped beam adjusted to a right-hand instead of a left-hand bias before you cross the Channel.

Apart from this point, your car needs no more preparation than it requires for any other long journey, although it is probably wise to ask the manufacturer for a list of agents abroad. A broken windscreen can mar a holiday and it is a good idea to take a temporary one rolled up in the boot. These emergency screens are made of plastic and, though they compress into a small package, they allow you excellent visibility when fitted in place of a broken glass windscreen.

Finally, don't forget your GB plate!

27

NOW FOR THE TEST

Having come with us this far, and if you are not already a member of the Institute of Advanced Motorists, you must be wondering if you have developed the ability to pass the advanced driving test.

In short, how good a driver are you? Very expert, perhaps, but are you sure? You may have passed the Government's driving test with ease at your first attempt. This, however, is a very basic, elementary examination. Passing it should be merely the beginning of your motoring career – the starting point in the acquisition of mature driving skills. Happily, most motorists realise this and there comes a time when they want to reassure themselves that their skill is developing along the right lines.

This is what the Institute of Advanced Motorists is all about. Founded in 1956, it is a non-profit-making organisation registered as a charity and dedicated to the promotion of road safety by encouraging motorists to take a pride in their driving. By taking the Institute's test, drivers can measure the progress they have made since throwing away their L-plates.

The test, which lasts for about 90 minutes, is something which any motorist of reasonable experience and skill should be able to pass without difficulty. But whether the candidates pass or fail, they learn a great deal from the Class One police drivers who conduct the tests on routes located all over Britain.

Skill with responsibility – that is what the IAM aims to promote. If every driver had the ability to pass the IAM test and the self-discipline to employ its standards at all times, there would be a dramatic drop in the number of road casualties, which average 330,000 a year at present. You have to pass the test to become a member of the Institute.

The Institute was founded by motorists from all walks of life with the common aim of making our roads safer by raising driving standards. It is controlled by a Council elected as a result of their expertise in various spheres of motoring. They represent accident prevention authorities, medicine, the motor industry and trade, driving schools, magistrates, the motoring Press, other motoring organisations, and the Institute's own area Groups.

The IAM's activities have been endorsed by successive Transport Ministers since it started. As an expert organisation its opinions concerning driving safety matters are regularly sought by the Government. Indeed, one of its main aims is to represent the views of skilled, responsible motorists to the authorities. To this end, each new member of the Institute becomes a valuable addition to the campaign for better driving and safer roads.

The advanced test has been adopted by the Army at home and abroad, and by more than 350 companies as a stringent check on the driving skill of staff using company-owned vehicles. So far, some 250,000 motorists have taken the test and 70 per cent of them have passed and become members of the Institute. Of these successful drivers one in five is a woman, with a success rate in the test similar to the men.

So what does the test involve? We'll start by looking at a typical test route. Each of the routes in Britain measures about 35–40 road miles and incorporates road conditions of all kinds, including congested urban areas, main roads, narrow country lanes, and residential streets. You are not expected to give a display of fancy driving; on the contrary, you should handle your car in the steady, workmanlike way in which you drive every day. The examiners don't, for example, expect exaggeratedly slow speeds or excessive signalling. They do want to see candidates observe all speed limits and drive with due regard to road, traffic and weather conditions. They will also want to see you driving briskly and to ensure that you are not afraid to cruise at the legal limit when circumstances permit – progress with safety.

You will be asked to reverse around a corner and to make a hill start. There will be one or two spot checks on your powers of observation. There are no trick questions in the test and no attempts to catch you out. You are not even required to give a running commentary at any time (although you are free to do so if you wish, to make extra clear your ability to 'read the road').

Here in greater detail are some of the points the examiners look for and comment on in their test reports:

Acceleration

Smooth and progressive? Excessive or insufficient? Is acceleration used at the right time and place?

Braking

Smooth and progressive or late and fierce? Are the brakes used in conjunction with mirror and signals? Are road, traffic and weather conditions taken into account?

Clutch control

Are engine and road speeds properly co-ordinated when changing gear? Does the candidate slip or ride the clutch? Does he coast with the clutch disengaged?

Gearchanging

Is it a smooth change action, without jerking? If automatic transmission is fitted, does the driver make full use of it?

Use of gears

Are the gears correctly selected and used? Is the right gear selected before reaching a hazard?

Steering

Is the wheel held correctly with the hands at the quarter-to-three or ten-to-two positions? Does the driver pass the wheel through his hands? Use of the 'cross arms' technique, except when manoeuvring in confined spaces, is not recommended.

Driving position

Is the candidate alert or does he slump at the wheel? Does he nonchalantly rest an arm on the door while driving?

Observation

Does he 'read' the road ahead and show a good sense of anticipation? Does he show the ability to judge speed and distance?

Concentration
Does the driver keep his attention on the road? Does he allow himself to be distracted easily?

Maintaining progress
Bearing in mind the road, traffic and weather conditions, does the driver keep up a reasonable pace and maintain good progress?

Obstruction
Is the candidate careful not to obstruct other vehicles, by driving too slowly, taking up the wrong position on the road, or failing to anticipate and react correctly to the traffic situation ahead?

Positioning
Does the driver keep to the correct part of the road, especially when approaching and negotiating hazards?

Lane discipline
Does he keep to the appropriate lane? Is he careful not to straddle white lines?

Observation of road surfaces
Does the driver keep an eye on the road surface, especially in bad weather, and does he watch out for slippery conditions?

Traffic signals
Are signals, signs and road markings observed, obeyed and approached correctly? Does the driver show courtesy at pedestrian crossings?

Speed limits and other legal requirements
Are they observed? The examiner cannot condone breaches of the law.

Overtaking
Is this carried out safely and decisively, maintaining the right distance from other vehicles and using the mirror, signals and gears correctly?

Hazard procedure and cornering
Are road and traffic hazards coped with properly? Are bends and corners taken in the right manner?

Mirror
Does the candidate frequently use the mirror? Does he use it in conjunction with his signals and before changing speed or course?

Signals
Are turn indicator signals – and hand ones when needed – given at the right place and in good time? Are the horn and headlight flasher used in accordance with the Highway Code?

Restraint
Does the candidate show reasonable restraint – but not indecision – at the wheel?

Consideration
Is sufficient consideration and courtesy shown to other road users?

Car sympathy
Does he treat the car with care? Does he overstress it, perhaps by revving the engine needlessly or by fierce braking?

Manoeuvring
Finally, are manoeuvres, such as reversing, performed smoothly and competently?

At the end of your test your examiner will, after announcing the result, give you an expert view of your skill and responsibility at the wheel. There may be praise and certainly constructive criticism will be offered – the Institute aims at being entirely honest with you. Occasionally, for instance, a driver is found to have developed a potentially dangerous fault of which he is completely unaware. A quiet word from the examiner may help him correct it. You will not be failed for minor faults.

Who can take the test?   Anyone with a full British or EEC driving licence providing that he has not been convicted of a serious traffic offence in the last three years. You can take the test in almost any car which you provide yourself, on most vans and trucks, and certain three-wheelers.

How about disabled drivers?   Disabled drivers are welcome as candidates provided they use a suitably adapted car.

Where can I take the test?   Probably close to your home. The Institute has a nationwide network of test routes, as you will see from the list on the following pages. The examiner will meet you at a pre-arranged rendezvous. Tests are available from Monday to Friday.

Can I prepare?   Yes, of course. There are many books available on advanced driving, among them the manuals we mentioned earlier. Also, some professional driving instructors *may* coach pupils up to the standard of the advanced test. In addition, you can ask your local council's road safety officer for details of advanced driving courses in your area, and in many areas the Institute's own local groups (details from IAM) can help you to prepare through their Associate Group Member Schemes.

Who are the examiners?   They are all holders of the Class One Police driving certificate. This means that they have passed the stiffest test of driving ability in Britain – the Police examination for traffic patrol drivers.

When you pass . . .   the test and become a member of the IAM these are among the benefits you can have:

Badge   The right to display the Institute's badge on your car, providing visible proof of the standard you have set yourself.

Insurance   An introduction to motor insurers who may, subject to a satisfactory proposal, give special terms.

Magazine   A motoring magazine, *Milestones*, is published every four months, and is produced especially for IAM members and written by and for people who take a keen interest in driving and cars.

Social activities   The chance to meet other men and women who share your outlook on motoring, if you decide to join one of the

Institute's local groups and take part in the road safety driving and social events which they organise.

The Institute is at IAM House, 359–365 Chiswick High Road, London, W4 4HS
Telephone: 01-994-4403 (24-hour answering service).

LIST OF TEST ROUTES

The following is a list of test routes operated by the IAM at the time of going to press. If you are in any doubt, the Institute will confirm which current route is most convenient for you.

Aberdeen	Huddersfield	Sheffield
Ayr	Hull	Shetlands
Bangor	Inverness	Shrewsbury
Bedford	Ipswich	Southampton
Belfast	Isle of Man	Staines
Birkenhead	Isle of Wight	Stoke-on-Trent
Birmingham	King's Lynn	Swansea
Blackpool	Leeds	Swindon
Bolton	Leicester	Taunton
Bournemouth	Lichfield	Truro
Brighton	Lincoln	Tunbridge Wells
Bristol	Liverpool	Wakefield
Burton-on-Trent	Luton	Watford
Cambridge	Maidstone	Wick
Canterbury	Manchester	Widnes
Cardiff	Mansfield	Windsor
Carlisle	Middlesbrough	Wolverhampton
Chelmsford	Newark	Worcester
Cheltenham	Newcastle	Worksop
Chester	Newmarket	Worthing
Colwyn Bay	Norwich	Yeovil
Coventry	Nottingham	**London**
Crawley	Omagh	Barnes
Crewe	Oxford	Crystal Palace
Derby	Penrith	Harrow
Dorchester	Peterborough	Wanstead
Dundee	Peterhead	**West Germany**
Edinburgh	Plymouth	*(HM Forces and Brit-*
Elgin	Portsmouth	*ish nationals only)*
Exeter	Preston	Bielefeld
Glasgow	Reading	Gutersloh
Grantham	Rotherham	Hanover
Grimsby	Salisbury	Paderborn
Guildford	Scunthorpe	Rheindahlen
Hereford		

Warning signs

Distance to stop sign ahead

Road narrows on right side (left side if symbol reversed)

Single file in each direction

Road wide enough for only one line of traffic

Dual carriageway ends

Pedestrian crossing ahead

Slippery road

Height limit (eg low bridge)

Cross Roads

Staggered junction

Road narrows on both sides

Traffic merges from right

Steep hill upwards

Uneven road

Level crossing with gate or barrier

Roundabout

Side Road

Double bend first to left (may be reversed)

Two way traffic straight ahead

The gradient may be expressed as a percentage eg 1:10 = 10%

Hump bridge

Level crossing without gate or barrier

Headroom at hazard

— Available width of headroom at hazard —

T Junction

Bend to right (or left if symbol reversed)

Traffic merges from left

Two way traffic crosses one way road

Traffic signals ahead

Opening or swing bridge

Change to opposite carriageway ahead (may be reversed)

Single file traffic

Single track road

GIVE WAY
50 yds

**Distance to
give way sign ahead**

School

**Children going
to and from school**

Patrol

School crossing ahead

(some signs have
amber lights which
flash when the patrol
is operating)

Fallen tree

**Other danger
(plate indicates
nature of danger)**

**Quayside or
river bank**

Loose chippings

**Accompanied horses
crossing the road**

**Right hand lane
closed ahead
(symbols may be reversed)**

**Low flying aircraft or
sudden aircraft noise**

**Risk of falling
or fallen rocks**

Cattle

Wild animals

**Location of level crossing
without gate or barrier**

**Sharp deviation of route to left
(or right if chevrons reversed)**

Roadworks

Safe height
16'-6"

**Overhead electric cable
plate indicates maximum
safe headroom available**

Signs giving orders

STOP

**Present sign
Stop and give way**

STOP

**New sign
Stop and give way**

**Turn left ahead
(right if symbol reversed)**

**Turn left
(right if symbol reversed)**

**Keep left
(right if symbol reversed)**

**Mini roundabout (roundabout
circulation give way to traffic
from immediate right)**

**Vehicles may pass
either side to reach
same destination**

GIVE
WAY

**Give way to traffic
on major road**

No entry for vehicular traffic

School crossing patrol

Ahead only

One way traffic

No right turn

No left turn

No U turns

No overtaking

Waiting restrictions apply

No stopping on main carriageway ('clearway')

Mon-Sat
8 am-6·30 pm

No loading
Mon-Fri
8·00-9·30 am
4·30-6·30 pm

Times of limited waiting (above) no loading/unloading (below)
(if no days are shown the restriction applies every day including Sundays and Bank Holidays)

Mon-Sat
8am-6pm
Waiting Limited
to 20 minutes
Return prohibited
within 40 minutes

Times of limited waiting

No stopping
except buses
7am-7pm

Protected bus stop

No cycling

Route available only for pedal cyclists

All vehicles prohibited

No pedestrians

All motor vehicles prohibited

All motor vehicles except solo motor cycles, scooters and mopeds prohibited

Motor cycles prohibited

Buses and coaches prohibited

3 tons

Goods vehicles over specified unladen weight prohibited

Horse drawn vehicles prohibited

← 32 → feet

Vehicle or combination of vehicles exceeding length indicated prohibited

10 TONS

Vehicles (including load) exceeding the figure indicated prohibited

14'-6"

Vehicles exceeding height indicated prohibited

2 TONS

Vehicles (including load) exceeding the weight indicated on axle prohibited

7·6"

Vehicles exceeding width indicated prohibited

30

Maximum speed

National speed limit applies

30

Minimum speed

End of minimum speed

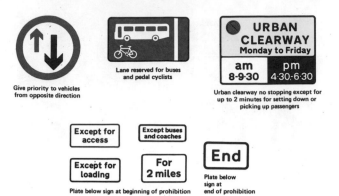

Give priority to vehicles
from opposite direction

Lane reserved for buses
and pedal cyclists

Urban clearway no stopping except for
up to 2 minutes for setting down or
picking up passengers

Except for
access

Except buses
and coaches

Except for
loading

For
2 miles

End

Plate below
sign at
end of prohibition

Plate below sign at beginning of prohibition

Other information signs

Priority over vehicles
from opposite direction

Pedal cyclists only

Advance warning
of no through road

No through road
for vehicular
traffic

Direction to service area with
fuel, parking, cafeteria and
restaurant facilities

Bus Stop

'Count down' markers at exit from motorway
(each bar represents 100 yards to the exit)

Parking place

Meter
ZONE
Mon-Fri
8·30 am - 6·30 pm
Saturday
8·30 am - 1·30 pm

Entrance to
controlled parking
zone

Zone
ENDS

Direction signs

Signs on approaches to junctions—green background on primary routes white background on other routes. Blue bordered signs show local places. Routes in brackets are turnings off road indicated.

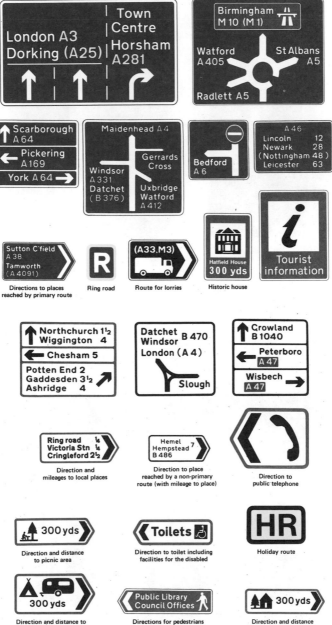

Light signals

Green arrow — if the way is clear vehicles may proceed but only in the direction indicated by the arrow

Pedestrians wait

Lane closed to traffic facing the signal

Lane open to traffic facing the signal

Flashing green — <u>don't</u> start to cross lights are about to change

Pedestrians cross with care

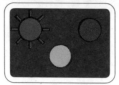

Level crossing stop at flashing red lights

Flashing amber — <u>give</u> way to pedestrians only proceed if crossing is clear

Road and kerb markings

Lane line   Centre line   Warning line

Give way lines across the mouth of a minor road

Stop lines at stop sign

Give way signs and lines with advance warning triangle

Stop line at light signals and places where police control traffic

No crossing

No crossing solid line if nearer to driver than broken line

Do not enter marked area

SCHOOL — KEEP — CLEAR

To indicate to vehicular traffic that part of the Carriageway outside a school which should be kept clear of stationary vehicles

Small yellow marks on the kerb or road show places where loading and unloading is prohibited during:

every working day*

every working day and additional times*

any other periods*

Box junction
Do not enter the box junction if your exit road or lane from it is not clear. But you may enter the junction when you want to turn right and are prevented from doing so only by oncoming traffic

Yellow lines along road show places where waiting (except for loading and unloading) is prohibited including on verges during:

every working day*

every working day and additional times*

any other periods*

Road-side plates show times when waiting or loading and unloading is prohibited

*May include Sundays and Bank Holidays

*On the approach zig-zags, drivers must not overtake the moving motor vehicle nearest the crossing, or the leading vehicle which has stopped to give way to a pedestrian on the crossing.

Mini roundabout

Zebra crossing zig-zags give advance warning of the presence of a crossing. They also mark an area where vehicles must not:
a) overtake*
b) wait or park
Pedestrians should not cross on the zig-zag areas. They should always use the crossing.